A
Wonderful
Change

by

Dara Mayhoe

Copyright © May 2019 Dara Mayhoe

All rights reserved. no part of this book may be reproduced in any form, stored in a retrieval system, or transmitted in any form by any means; electronic, mechanical, photocopying, recording or otherwise without the prior written permission of approval from the author, Dara Mayhoe

All rights reserved

Illustration; Kevin "Gump" Wolfrom Jr.
Gump14.kw@gmail.com

A Wonderful Change

A WORD OF THANKS

Writing a book is harder than I thought and more rewarding than I ever imagined. None of this would be possible without God who is the joy of my salvation, my rock and my redeemer.

With most sincere regards to my editor Mary Harris, it would have been very challenging to complete this project without these you. You stepped in and helped me understand how to tell my story in a way that keeps the reader engaged and captivated with the book. Thank you so much!

To my incredibly talented illustrator Kevin "Gump" Wolfrom Jr. What an awesome experience seeing you turn my idea into a reality! Kevin is truly a professional artist who served my project with intention to provide complete client satisfaction!! Thank you so much!

Dara,

A Wonderful Change

DEDICATION

To you, my reader…..

Be encouraged as you read my story. I want you to know that whatever you're going through could change for your advantage. Perhaps you will share my story with someone facing similar challenges with hope that they too will have a chance at transformation, but only by faith, God's grace, His mercy and favor.

I am here to witness that those things that are meant to destroy us can actually catapult a believer into places only dreams can take you. Each story recorded in this book were actual events that took place in my life. The recollected accounts of misfortune, abuse, setbacks and heartaches are followed by nothing but victorious experiences and miracles.

This book was written to be an inspiration to many but as you read the pages my only desire is that it is an inspiration to you!

With much love and sincere regard,

Dara Mayhoe
Author

EDITORS NOTE

As an author the art of reading at times can be very challenging. It's kind of like baking a box cake and attempting to serve it to Chef Gordon Ramsey or Martha Stewart... sometimes it just doesn't go over too well. This can be equally challenging as an editor during the creative process because you must maintain the writers voice while ensuring that the readers have a clear picture of what the author is attempting to convey.

Dara Mayhoe has truly delivered an insightful, inspirational, informative piece of written work! There were moments that I had to wipe the tears from my eyes at the level of raw honesty that she has chosen to share with her readers. There were many moments that my cup of coffee became increasingly better as I read her manuscript, intaking each sentence, word by word and line by line ensuring that I was grasping the full content of what needed to be delivered. There were many moments where I as a woman, a mother, a survivor myself needed to stop and thank God for allowing me to partake in bringing her work to life.

As a professional black business woman Dara pulled my coat tail, warmed my heart and created a desire in me to become greater, love harder, believe more and accept all that life has to offer IF I am willing to work for it... Great JOB Dara! I am excited to see the next steps for you.

With Honor and Respect,
Mary A Love-Harris Chief Editor- GemStones Publishing House, LLC
A Wonderful Change

Acknowledgments

Thanking God for his grace and mercy, I don't even want to know where I would be, He has kept me through it all!

My parents Sanford Watts and Tondra Larkins, two significant parts of my life! Dad you have shown me how to bounce back and you are the absolute best Grandfather to my children!

Mama I love you and I'm grateful for the love you have given me despite our hardships throughout life, God has kept us together and still working on our behalf! Won't he do it?!

To my best friend Janielle Houston the only friend who stuck with me through it ALL good, bad, happy or sad you were there to hold my hand- literally! I love you girl!

My Brother, Delvonce Larkins and Sister, DiRen Larkins I love you both tremendously you all have witnessed some of my craziest days I'm so grateful I can call you both my siblings! Thank you for your love!

My church family The Bread House Main Campus of Lansing. A ministry who has stood with my family 100%, a place where spiritual growth has taken place in my life by the power of God. I owe a lot to my pastor Bishop Alfred

P. Singleton and First Lady Vivian Singleton your support is immeasurable!

My sassy and classy mother in love Juanita M.Williams who has embraced me since day one.. okay well since about a year after marrying her Son and having her Granddaughter! Lol don't hurt me Mom I love you so much! Truly one of my greatest friends!

To all of our children whether by birth or by marriage all of you have inspired me to be the very best version of me. Mark Jr (resting in paradise) Tiffany, Eric, Keith, Mardwane, Brionna and Micah thank you for sharing your Dad with me, my life is so much better than before! I love you all!

It has been the greatest experience to birth three children from my womb.

DeAndre, you have taught me to love unconditionally you have expressed the epitome of true love. I love you Son!

Elijah, you've been my rider and My Bodyguard thank you for loving me when I have been hard to love and hard on you. I love you Son!

Victoria the princess of our family and my real life doll you are a rare gem, more precious than rubies. I love you sweet pea!

And lastly, to my amazing husband Mark... You are truly my prince charming, my knight in shining armor, my dream come true, my absolute greatest Inspiration! I am who I am today by the power of God used through you to enhance my life. I could never repay you for the impact you've had on me. You are my forever one and only true love, best friend and soulmate. I love you sweetheart!

A Wonderful Change

CONTENTS

1. In the Beginning — 1
2. G-Baby — Pg. 7
3. Wild & Rebellious — Pg. 20
4. Love & Lock-Up — Pg. 24
5. Hustle & Blow — Pg. 37
6. Sumthn' Like an Ike & Tina Remix — Pg. 50
7. Baby Steps… I'm gettin' there — Pg. 68
8. A Wonderful Change — Pg. 76
9. Make it Last Forever — Pg. 82
10. A Family Reunion — Pg. 87

A Wonderful Change A Wonderful Change

A Wonderful Change

Chapter 1

In the Beginning

Dara Larkins, a beautiful baby girl born from the union of a 30-year-old tall, handsome brown-skinned man and a 24-year-old fine, flattering young lady. Two people who were not living up to their potential at the time, but in their attempt to find their way found each other. The relationship lasted maybe a total of six months but nonetheless, I was born and shortly after they stopped seeing each other, my father moved to Chicago. From then on out, it was child support and random "pop up" visits.

My mother did the best she could. It was time for her to strategize taking care of three children that did not have their father present in their lives, no man in her life, and her means of support was a minimal income that couldn't stretch too far.

Around the age of 6 months old I became ill all of a sudden. I was diagnosed with spinal meningitis and fluid on my brain. I underwent emergency surgery but in the process I developed a severe fever of 105 degrees and the doctors informed my mother that the condition of my health would leave me seriously handicapped, or in a vegetative state due to the brain damage this illness would cause.

My mother during this time was truly led by faith. I know this from her personal recollection of accounts that she prayed her way through that situation. Well, "By HIS stripes I am healed" (Isaiah 53:5 New American Standard Bible)

My mother began to experience severe depression around the time that I reached age 7. She was always sad, tired or lethargic and as a child I always wondered why she was always so sad???

These times were always tough! I remember moving a lot for many years; we either were going from shelter to shelter, living with people or moving into a different, "new" apartment. Things were never stable or consistent for us. If we lived in one spot for more than a year or two it was record breaking.

After years of bouncing around somewhere in the process things started getting better, my mom had gotten married! What a nice guy he was to us, we finally had a dad in the house and fortunately he was someone who had a lot of respect for my sister, brother and me. He was a real dream come true, a hard-working nice guy who truly adored my mother. Sadly, her depression became worse and worse and she began to drink heavily, become violent and angry. Our stepdad was an alcoholic too so she would be drunk and angry, and he would be drunk and crying. I remember lots of sleepless nights hearing them drink and argue, eventually she would leave, go to the club and my sister and I would hear him up all night crying until her return. My Stepdad was a good guy, but he also had some underlying issues as well. They both needed help!

My mother grew increasingly edgy, mean and more depressed, to the point of being admitted to the psychiatric hospital for days of surveillance. We were scared for our mother, we didn't know what was going on with her, but we knew it was really serious. It was hard knowing she was there, we wanted to help her so badly but couldn't.

Around the age of 10 or 12 the dream come true ended… the ride was over; my mom and her husband got a divorce. It was only so long that they were going to make it considering the issues that the both of them had. It was back to poverty for us, and single parenting for my mom. I hated seeing her depressed, the pressures of single parenting began to weigh heavily on her, and we could see it every single day. Even as a child I knew she wasn't necessarily mad at me or her other children, but it was hard for her to find peace and happiness with the challenges that she was facing.

As a child who was being forced to quickly grow up, I began to think of ways to put a little money in my pocket without having to bug my mom about the stuff we wanted. Even if it was just a snack, I was at the age where I was tired of being broke and I needed to come up with a plan.

As I watched the outside world I began to yearn for more financial freedom. It seemed like everyone around me lived comfortably and I resented going to visit friends at their nice warm homes where it appeared that they had everything they needed. I was determined to get my slice of that! I wanted the nice gym shoes and extra money for lunch too! I was bold.

I wasn't afraid of much at this time and I felt that It was time for me to establish a hustle petty enough for a kid my age, I believe I was 11.

Ah-ha. In comes the "5-finger discount". The trick to this hustle was that I was unsuspecting, wellmannered and had a cute little baby face.

I was doing little stuff like hitting up the local grocery store for cases of bubble gum and candy bars, and then I would turn around and sell it to school kids for twenty-five cents. I always came home with at least five or ten dollars at the end of the school day. Finally, it felt good having money in my pocket but even at my young age, I knew at some point I'd get caught...and I did! Here my sister and I were at the store. She was with me because she just liked tagging along, but ME? Dara? was picking up cases of candy like I had the right to walk out the store with it or something. 10 years old and had just committed my first crime and got caught! Thank God the police did not arrest us, but my mom handled the punishment. Mom whipped my behind really good as deserved. That whipping started from the grocery store and it lasted all the way until we got back to our home. I was so embarrassed, there were so many of my friends outside as we approached the house. All of the kids were the same ones I had been selling the candy to. I had quickly gone from the cool candy peddler to the laughingstock!

That wasn't enough to sit me down though, that money in my pocket had felt good and I was willing to risk it again; just not at that store.

Before I knew it I was panhandling, pickpocketing and stealing out of purses. This was the next best hustle, and I had to get it. For a child, this was a guaranteed way of getting a lot more money than from just "pushing candy". I never really thought of the consequences all I could think of was having the extra money my mom didn't have.

At the peak of my delinquent behavior I started going blind in my left eye.

I only had about 40 to 50 percent of my vision. I can remember wearing an ugly brown patch over my eye, with thick coke bottle glasses. The kids used to tear me up at school. Teasing me by calling me "Slick Rick" who at that time was a well-known rapper who only had one eye, a pirate and many other mean names that demeaned my physical appearance.

I hated going to school. I would fake being sick or I would get into fist fights just so I didn't have to go to school. Before I knew it, I was just as depressed as mom was. I started cutting my wrists. I figured if someone noticed the scars they would give me the special attention I felt I need to make up for the teasing and bullying I endured at school.

I was dealing with my blindness the best I could but then all of a sudden we noticed that my hair had started falling out too! It was all the way bad for me. It fell out so fast that all I had left was the perimeter of my hairline. My mom took me back to the doctor where we learned that I had Alopecia, an immune deficiency that attacks the follicles of the hair due to severe stress.

My mama did all she could to help me with the situation from special doctors, to wigs, to scarves and earrings you name it she tried it but to no avail, this only furthered my downward spiral. This was the straw that broke my back. The stress, the teasing, the pressure, the lack from birth until now birthed a Savage! With the kids at school tormenting me so many questions started rolling in.. did I have Cancer? Did I get burned? Was it a bad perm that made my hair fall out?

These, along with many other dumb questions that they could think of became the norm of my days. I grew vehemently angry by the comments and remarks, some of the kids would even sneak up from behind and pull my wig off! Finally, I had had enough. I was ready to fight anyone, and everyone who got in my way!

Chapter 2

G-Baby

12-year-old Dara was a serious force to be reckoned with. As I grew into myself, or at least the street, no nonsense, taking care of herself at age 12 self I learned to be defensive. Unfortunately, being defensive consisted of me fighting a lot and that always got me kicked out of school. I would be out of school many days and hit the streets, but considering my hustle was solid it was worth the risk. As I said, risky but solid because I still hadn't forgotten the way my mama tore my behind up for stealing. If she knew I was hustling the neighborhood folks she'd kill me!

One day I came home from school and all of our belongings were on the side of the road, it had been a little while since we had dealt with an eviction, so this was a shock! After splitting up going to stay with various family members we reunited after a few months and moved into the projects across town.

That move totally killed my grind. I went from the hustle & bustle of downtown workers and students to more broke people that were just like us, as well as drunks and dope fiends.

I hated the new place. It didn't take me long to want to get out of there, and although I couldn't get out physically I had to get out mentally and that avenue was provided by exploring with boys! I thought I was ready to venture out. I had my eye on this particular kid. I was about 12 years old fast, furious and curious.
I was never shy so going after what I wanted was never an issue. One night I decided to sneak out to a house party while my mom was out doing her thing. The party was lit and there I was in a dark room, alone with a boy and ended up going too far. Just like that! I lost my innocence in a moment of exploration and wanting to feel accepted.

I couldn't believe it, the most precious thing I held on to was gone. What a sad situation and prime example of what happens when we throw our precious children to the wolves. I felt so dirty, so low, guilty and ashamed, of all of the bad things I had ever done, this was by far the worst.

My mom ended up finding out, I was so afraid. I knew things were not going to be pretty. From that point on I was treated like another woman in the house. We couldn't get along for anything!

We argued constantly; I became untrustworthy to her. Everyone in the projects knew what happened. I wasn't trusted and I was embarrassed by the reputation I had just acquired.

Life just became an abusive, tumultuous mess. Honestly I was not the fast girl that I had gained the reputation for being. I was a sad little girl who was affected by depression and low self-esteem just as my mother was dealing with.

Attention from boys and cutting myself seemed to bring the attention I was looking for, but it didn't do anything for the crazy relationship I had with my mom. We fought constantly, to the point of waking up one day living with some strange lady who I had NOTHING in common with and a bunch of kids who had behavior issues and came from broken homes just like me.

Yup, I was in Foster Care. A melting pot of damaged kids who just wanted to feel loved and accepted by the ones who brought them in the world!

Honestly it wasn't so bad, this lady only wanted a check & really didn't care about what I was doing. She took pretty good care of me. I got a monthly check that she would split with me. It felt good to have a sense of allowance and freedom. Home was the farthest thing from my mind. I did what I wanted to do, and she was fine with that. She never set rules.

My days consisted of skipping school, roaming the streets, drinking Cisco with my friends at the bus stop and smoking weed right on her front porch. Life was great!...so it seemed.

My life quickly became consumed with counseling, teen group sessions at the county building and supervised visits with my mom. I hated it, half of the time I wouldn't even show up. I would leave and say she never showed up, I was resentful and hoped they never sent me back home.

Being in Foster care took me to a new school, new friends and new people to be teased by. I was known for fighting my way through the bullying and doing stupid stuff to prove I was tough!

I found myself kicked out of school, this time for setting a false fire emergency and fighting. My foster mom and I ended up having an argument and I was moved to a new foster home. I didn't care, she had about seven kids, one of which was a REAL fire starter and I didn't want to be around if the kid set the house on fire. I left that foster home without incident.

This new foster mom was more on my level, she was young and cool! I loved being there, the family embraced me immediately and they were good to me. There was a little more structure, but I still had room to do what I wanted to do. While I didn't aspire to be home with my mother, I did begin to miss her and especially my sister tremendously!

Although I was in a foster home I was with a great family and it gave me another perspective on what family could be like, other than what I knew. They were a God-fearing family that I was safe with. As it turned out they knew my family very well.

I was blending into a rather large family of people who really seemed to love each other. I would daydream and imagine being asked to stay with them forever, that would have been a dream come true.

However, I was still furious and curious, sneaking around with boys, smoking and skipping school. It wasn't long before my foster mom found out. I will never forget the day I overheard the conversation asking for me to be removed. I knew it was over then. My time with that family had served its purpose. My season there had ended.

I was remorseful, I wanted to prove myself, but it was too late, I had burned that bridge and it was time to move on.

I bagged up and made my way on down to Foster home number three. All I could do was think about the situation I had gotten myself into again. I felt rejected. My family didn't want me and now foster homes were kicking me out. I contemplated running away but I didn't have anywhere to go.

I was so tired of moving around, meeting new people and living with complete strangers.

I absolutely hated the next home. This foster care mother was depressed, hardly ever talked and always beat the heck out of the kids. The house was always dark and gloomy. She would sit around on the phone all day gossiping, or in the kitchen cooking for all of the kids. She really wasn't so bad but there was always just an eerie feeling in the house. Her biological daughters hated me and tormented me calling me all kinds of rejects and whores, always telling me their mom only wanted me there for the check. They were completely irritated that I was there, I was irritated just being there so the feeling was mutual. I felt like they were trying to get me to run away. It wasn't much different from the other foster homes as far as the rules. She really didn't care where we went as long as we were back by 9. I used this to my advantage by still sneaking to see boys and also sneaking back home to spend time with my sister. I also spent a lot of time at the local drop in center. I looked for any and every reason to stay away until it was time to go back before dark. This whole foster care thing was starting to weigh heavily, I had a yearning to go back home with my mother and my sister.

One night I was just hanging around the neighborhood corner store, I decided to go in and get a few hair care products on the "five-finger discount". I had always heard about the owner being a pervert, but I never paid much attention to it, being young and naive.

A Wonderful Change

Unfortunately, I found out that rumor was true! He probably couldn't wait to get his nasty hands on me. I'm only thirteen and he's every bit of fifty!!! On this day I was in the store behaving normally, looking for the products I had come in to get. The store was small but not that small. I bent over to get something on the bottom shelf that's when he came up behind me, grabbed me by my 13-year-old hips and, gave a forceful thrust from his groin to my bottom!

Oh God! I took off running for my life! I told my foster mom, but I don't really remember anything much coming out of it. I recall running in the house frantically, she had a house full of company and barely listened to anything I said. She thought I was lying, after all, they knew him. He had been around for years perhaps nothing like that had ever happened with any of the other children she had raised but it had just happened to me and I wanted her to care!

I felt so low, so alone…my mother didn't want me, the foster parents didn't care and now I'm being exposed to more people who saw no value in me. What's next?

Here we are! Time for court! I had been in foster care for a little over a year and it's time to re-evaluate progress between my mother and me.

Something obviously worked in my mom's favor! I went back home, and things were great!.. for a little while. Then, we started back to the arguing we were doing all of the time before as usual. I felt like she didn't want me there. That was no insult because I didn't want to be any way.

The feelings I had before of missing my mom and home were gone! I absolutely hated being home. I hung out more and more which made the relationship between my mother and I aggressive again. I was constantly fighting at school because I was angry at home and the school kids were going to catch my frustration, ESPECIALLY if they got in my way.

I was in the 9th grade when I went back home. My sister and I were finally in high school together! That was a highly anticipated time in my life at that point, I was highly protective of my big sister and I wanted to be close to her.

At that point I had acquired a strong reputation for fighting. Being tough was my way of gaining respect for myself, I had never felt respected by anyone. All I wanted for people to know was- "Don't mess with me or my sister".

She was the oldest and technically my "big sister" but I was sensitive and protective of her. She was beautiful, well liked, smart and employed. She avoided fighting as much as possible but that didn't mean she didn't have haters.

I was already angry at the world and felt no one ever stood up for me, it was time to show my sister loyalty. The same loyalty I yearned waiting for someone to come get me out of foster care.

Some of the high school girls didn't like her. She was stuck up in their eyes. I was always boisterous about having my sisters back. The girls hated me because I never showed fear of them, sometimes I was intimidated but I never showed it.

I'll never forget walking down that narrow hall at Eastern High School. It was about three of them lined up on each side, all I could think was "They are really about to get me!" I always felt like they were going to "jump me" so I kept a pair of scissors in my hoodie at all times. They all jumped on me and had me on the ground, I can't recall how I was able to get up, but I jumped to my feet and brandished my scissors. One of the girls closest to me took off running down the stairs and I chased after her. I ran behind her as fast as I could, when I got outside there was no sign of the girl. That was a blessing for her because with the anger I was feeling I know I would've cut her. I am grateful to this day for how that situation ended.

I had already been in numerous petty fights and the school administration was sick of me. I was expelled from the entire school district and sent to an alternative school. I didn't care, I hated Eastern High School anyway, in fact I hated school!

The move to Alternative Education was even worse, that's where I was able to reconnect with all of my bad friends who couldn't prosper in traditional school either.

I was the cool "homegirl" that all of my boys saw as "Sis". I acted like the boys and looked very much like a "girly girl"

The guys trusted me and knew I was less suspecting than them. I was the "mule" if you want to call me that. We did everything from sell weed at school to trading guns. They paid me each job.

One day one of my boys asked me to hold his gun for the day, that wasn't anything unusual to me. I had a name to make, I wanted him to know I was "down", so I said yes! The day progressed and I am in my last class when all of a sudden at least 10 police officers and security guards approached me.

They didn't waste any time hand cuffing me and taking me into another room to pat me down and interrogate me. They somehow knew that I had the gun. They confiscated it and took me down to the police station. I couldn't believe the trouble I had just gotten myself into. Was it really worth it? Was this really the "cool" I was trying to be? As it turned out my homeboy's jealous girlfriend had ratted us out. She thought we had something personal going on, but it was all business.

Next thing I know both of us are in Juvenile detention with a felony count of carrying a concealed weapon. It didn't move me much, I had by this time learned how to quickly adjust. I was used to my life being disrupted, living with strange kids and adults.

Surprisingly the detention center was actually fun! I was able to make some reflections. I hadn't slowed down enough to look at my self-destructive ways before. I actually had an opportunity to act like a kid and do kid things like games and school, so it didn't feel like lock up to me.

They would have talent shows and karaoke, and for the first time I discovered my singing voice! I began to embrace singing and actually won a few contests while there. That felt so good for someone to give me a chance, to let my singing voice be heard.

No one really supported or mentored me during the time I was locked up, except for my Granny. She was a huge support in my life always there to help me through! I think I was in juvie around four months or so.

After my release I went to go stay with Granny, but I wasn't completely free, I was on probation and house arrest. I really couldn't go anywhere other than to school and back. That was cool though because on the inside I really wanted to change!

I knew I wanted to calm down, get back to Jesus and do well in school like some of my closest peers. My life was a mess, but I also had another set of friends who were making good choices and being raised in stable and loving homes. I reconnected with some of them and dropped all of my friends from the hood. It was time for a fresh new start, no more thug stuff.

I was kicked out of the entire school district, nowhere to attend public school. A decision had to be made. That's when Granny decided to put me in private school. That made me feel like she saw something in me, she knew there was something about me she had to cultivate. I wasn't just a thug, YOUNG REESEY, bad girl & baby G that I had been called all of my life and raised to believe I was. I was actually smart, spiritually inclined, intelligent beautiful and bold!

Private school was okay it was definitely a whole new world. I had to find an after-school activity to keep me out of the streets, so I became a cheerleader. Although I was making tremendous strides to do better , I was still sneaking around with boys and getting into petty trouble, but small changes were beginning to take place.

Two months of being on probation, my probation officer came to me with a proposition. I had been encouraged to apply for a position to take seat on a governmental committee. The way she was describing it sounded so prestigious! A juvenile justice committee that positively affected juvies like me!

I really couldn't understand why she was even asking me to do it I'm a kid fresh out of detention, on house arrest and probation and all of the other people were grown adults, Judges, lawyers & Juvenile Justice specialists. Why in the world would they want a lil hoodlum like me?! (Oh, ye of little faith) but God's favor was on my side!

I went along with the plan; I applied and was accepted as a "youth member". It was very interesting; I was able to see once again just how intelligent and important I was!

We were a committee organized by then Governor John Engler, working on behalf of JJDPA-Juvenile Justice and Delinquency Prevention Act. Our job was to make decisions to give money to different projects and programs in Michigan to advocate for Juvenile Justice and prevent delinquency.

I was at the height of my newfound confidence! Along with that position came some perks. I went to prestigious events and was catered to just as the Judges and other professionals there.

I also attended the Governor's Gubernatorial ball! I will never forget that experience! They had no clue they were mingling with some kid who was on probation and house arrest!

I'm grateful my probation officer saw something in me, I Think I was about 14 or 15.

Things seemed to be going pretty well but I couldn't stay out of trouble with boys, I was out past curfew often and violated my probation. Granny had let me get away with a lot, but this was the last time... she wasn't buying it anymore. Next thing I know, I'm headed back to stay with my mom, and I wasn't sure how long it was going to last-but here goes nothing!

On the onset, things were okay but as always it didn't take long for things to escalate between my mother and I who just could not get along. I was defiant, I was hurt and felt rejected Although I put myself in this situation, I was angry at Granny too! I never thought she would send me back home with my Mom.

I started staying out later and later, to the point I just stopped coming home at all.

Chapter 3

Wild and Rebellious

I found out about a runaway shelter, I called them and got a bed, so I didn't have to go home. My behavior became increasingly worse and at this time I thought I was grown; I was 16 with NO ONE to dictate my life. I was free to do what I wanted and when I wanted!

One day my friend Angela and I went to hang out with some guys, all of them were fine and had money.
Exactly what we were looking for!

We partied day in and day out until we both got kicked out of the runaway shelter for breaking curfew.

At that point I had pretty much burned my bridges with my Mom and my Granny, I reached out to my best friend and her mom.

They allowed me to come and stay with them for a while, although I was only 16 it was my plan to get a job and somehow find someone who would rent to me at that age.

I knew I had to come up with a plan quickly, I appreciated the hospitality but sleeping on their living room floor got played out fast. I remained friends with some of the guys Angela and I hung out with so I called up my homeboy G-Man to see if I could come and stay with him, but I could never get him to answer the phone. Several weeks Later I was watching the news and found out the same guys we were hanging out with had killed a girl! The news shared such gruesome details of the killing, even mentioning one of the guys we were hanging with was a cannibal and had eaten some of the victim's body!

I was so shook!! I couldn't believe it! That could have been me or one of my homegirls! Thank God for his covering!

I was trying to make it as best as I could staying with my friend and her mother. The situation was very uncomfortable, and I knew it wouldn't last long. Every night I thought of my next move.

Little did I know my next move was going to be sooner than I thought because I had to find a place to live with my soon to be born baby! Yes, I found out I was pregnant!

Finding out I was pregnant was one thing, but being pregnant by a loser, a player who already had another girl pregnant was another thing! I reached out to him to inform him of my pregnancy hoping and praying that my wildest dream of him accepting this crisis would be fulfilled. I was wrong! He denied it to the fullest! I felt so rejected and taken advantage of but that was nothing new. Honestly, I shouldn't have been dumb enough to be with him, this was the consequence. Although I knew I could've prevented the situation I was still angry, I was livid! I wasn't asking him to love me, I just wanted him to embrace his own seed and take care of what he created!

Meanwhile I was told I couldn't bring a baby in the house. I had to think fast and find a new place for me and baby to live. It seemed as if I was becoming a disgrace. The parents of some of my closest friends encouraged their kids to stay away from me, as if pregnancy was contagious. Most of my friends' parents adored me, but the pregnancy made them close doors that once welcomed me in. I always heard things like "trouble was following me, a dark cloud hung over my head & I was wasn't going to do much in life".

I had already been through Juvie, foster care, and a challenged homelife so what could be worse? So once again, I packed up as I was asked and went to live with my Granny. She was ready to give me a second chance. I thank God for her, she was always my home base.

I was trying as best as I could to stay in school, and I was actually doing good. My baby was growing inside of me and the reality of becoming a mother sooner than I imagined was quickly becoming more of a reality day by day. Trying to stay focused without dwelling on the fact that I'm going to have to "wing it" at parenthood all by myself. I stopped pursuing his support and let the courts deal with him.

I had actually acquired a boyfriend in the process. We will just call him Ricky. He was a good guy and seemed to really love me! Even though I was a lot to deal with, he helped me get through this pregnancy as best as he could. A seventeen-year-old athlete who had no clue how to deal with everything I had going on!

We dated the entire course of my pregnancy. Granny was always my backbone but for some reason she let me go, I think she felt as if she was enabling me, she had never let me go like that. Perhaps she finally got tired of me once and for good. Perhaps it was time for me to figure life out myself. I bounced around between shelters and friends for housing. I just couldn't shake the vicious cycle of homelessness & poverty. Nonetheless, Ricky was always there to help me as much as he could. His presence in my life was right on time. I had always felt alone; I didn't want to be alone with a baby.

It was time to have my baby! I will never forget it! Ricky was there for me the whole time, even during the C-section process. I remember laying there holding his hand. It was bitter-sweet. Bitter because the biological Father was somewhere not giving a care and sweet because my boyfriend was there giving all of the care in the world! Still, I was so afraid! I had brought a baby into this world with no idea how I should care for him. All I could do was pray I remember asking God to please help me, please stay with me!

A Wonderful Change

When the doctors pulled my baby from my womb I could tell something was terribly wrong. Everyone had looks of concern. I started to panic on the inside.

They cleaned my baby up and laid him on my chest. He looked unusual...something was wrong! It was as if his entire body was encased in a thick "pop bottle" plastic layer of skin. He couldn't move, he was stiff and couldn't even blink his eyes, the skin was so tight.

My baby was born with a serious skin condition Lamellar Ichthyosis, he needed full time special attention which meant I could not work.

My situation wasn't stable. That was my biggest challenge, being stable enough to actually care for a kid. My boyfriend saw how challenging it was for me to care for my baby and his needs while being homeless. He asked his mother if I could live with them and surprisingly enough she said yes!

I could not believe it I was so happy to finally have a sense of family after being in tumultuous, unstable situations all of my life! The idea of living in a functional home with my boyfriend helping me take care of my baby was absolutely mind-blowing!

This situation was actually working quite well I went to high school in the evenings and he was taking Community College courses in the daytime he was one year older than me.

Although I was in a good relationship with someone who obviously adored me and would do anything for me my pride began to get in the way. I couldn't see past the support; I could only see the opportunities that presented themselves.

My ugly duckling phase was over, and it went straight to my head. I started craving the attention I needed years before.

The years of alopecia, blindness, abuse, poverty and everything else that people teased me for were behind me! I started thinking much too highly of myself, one too many compliments went straight to my head.

I didn't have much regard for being in the relationship either, I was using him, and everyone knew it.

How selfish! What 17-year-old boy would want a girl with a baby who didn't belong to him? And whose parents would even go along with the idea of her living with them? That was so unlikely to happen, and I was about to blow a great opportunity!

I would leave my baby with my boyfriend to go hang out with other guys. They would pick me up or drop off gifts right in front of his house.

I didn't care, I hadn't experienced real love, never taught loyalty or even saw it. I was completely blind to identifying the blessings that were upon my life.

God had his hands on me in this situation, he sent someone to help but I was too selfish and blind to see it and nurture it.

It didn't take long for my boyfriend to find out! He loved me but he wasn't willing to be my fool! I didn't blame him; he was young with a whole future ahead of him. He was stressed by pressure of friends and family once the word got out about my infidelity.

It was time to accept what I had done and move on.
In that process I became homeless again. He and I actually tried to make things work although I was asked to leave. He still came to my rescue when I needed things for myself or my baby. For some reason he still felt a level of responsibility for us even though he wasn't my child's father.

Looking back on that part of my life it still blows my mind that all of that played out like that!

After staying at the shelter for about a month I finally got my first apartment! Me and my little baby were good to go!

I was so proud of my cute little efficiency apartment, until I realized it is severely infested with mice! Lord knows I am deathly terrified of mice! I didn't stay there long and found myself wiggling my way back home with my mother.

You know what I'm about to say next! "that didn't last long!" I moved out just as soon as I moved in! I ended up going to another shelter, this time it was a shelter for pregnant women, but they allowed me to come with my baby since he was so young. I believe he was just two or three months old. I was able to stay there for a while, roughly 5 months; just enough time for me to get on my feet, land a little nickel and dime job get help from the state of Michigan and get another apartment.

Life was awesome! I had my own place where no one could make me leave. Ricky and I were trying to work things out, but I continued to play mind games. Slowly but surely he was backing off, he knew I wasn't serious. I kept him for convenience. He and I both decided this thing wasn't going to work, and it was time to call it quits.

He was the closest thing I had to stability, but I knew no matter how hard I tried to keep him around, he wasn't the one for me.

My apartment was right on the west side and so were all of my friends. While Ricky and I dated I never had a lot of company because I knew he would come and break it up. He was the little bit of structure I needed. Now that we were apart I had free will to do whatever I wanted to do. Partying became my lifestyle; I maintained a nightly party house. I could barely keep a job and management was complaining of disturbance from my apartment.

My partying was so out of control. I started slacking on parenting and caring for my child who had serious special needs.

One day there was a knock at the door, and it was Protective Services coming to investigate my parenting. It was time to get to the bottom of my neglect. I was so afraid. I loved partying, but of course I wouldn't choose partying over my precious son! I had to hurry up and get it together!

I knew getting a job had to be first on my list, but they were low paying jobs. The thought of losing my baby scared me to my core but I was still immature. I really didn't see the harm in relying on the government to send that $400 check and $200 food stamps while I sat on my behind.. so, what if I missed a couple of appointments for my Son and it didn't matter if I let my bills pile up. I could just move somewhere else, that's all I knew. I was used to moving around when you couldn't pay the bills.

Chapter 4

"Love" & Lock-Up

Here we go again, kicked out of another apartment. It really wasn't too much of a crisis, going to a shelter was routine in these familiar situations and that's exactly what I did.

Most of the shelters were night shelters. My days consisted of dragging my baby all around town, visiting whoever I could until 6pm when I could go check back in at the shelter. I only needed to continue this game for a few days just to get the letter from the shelter verifying my homelessness and have

State pay for me to move into another apartment. I knew that game like the back of my hand.

I was able to land a small efficiency apartment; it was in a bad area, but it was mine. Drug dealers, gang members and prostitutes polluted the neighborhood. It really didn't matter much I felt right at home.
Slowly but surely I was becoming one of them.

It wasn't long before I was friends with some of the area hustlers. A few of them "put me on" in other words they gave me dope to sell and I'd pay them later. That gave me a head start to my new hustle. During that process I met a guy let's just call him "P" I thought he was "all that" he was a friend of my sister's ex-boyfriend who was a big-time Dope man. He was in the game as well, and even though I wasn't that physically attracted to him he dressed nice, had a lot of money & spoiled me!

The drawback was he was abusive, and I didn't see it coming. He was a "player" and didn't mind putting his hands on me!

It didn't take long for the sweet talking to wear off. He started hitting me for no reason. He became extremely jealous and controlling. He would assault me for any little reason. I had never been in this type of relationship before, once I got a taste of his abuse I planned to leave him. I was turned off and afraid to be with him. I stopped responding to his calls, he was a player so after a while he stopped calling anyway. It was a big adjustment with him gone. Being with him gave me access to a lot of money but it wasn't worth being his punching bag. I knew I would miss the money and little gifts but that was not worth the abuse, so I stood firm and never looked back to be with him again.

Bills started piling up and I really didn't want to sell dope, I stopped going to "re-cop" or get more dope and I didn't have a job or another hustle. I kept telling myself I didn't want to be broke and at that point I really didn't care how the money came. I just didn't want to have to kill anyone or sell dope.

The Dope Game just wasn't what I was cut out for. I was eyeballing everything(estimating weight) and was way off! It was too uncomfortable. I was very paranoid sitting in drug houses, and I hated "bleeding the block" which meant canvassing the neighborhood looking for dope fiends. I would be in sub-zero temperatures with five layers of clothing on hoping to run up on a couple of smokers or Petty dope boys looking for a double up. It was time to retire from this experience of being the dope girl, but I still needed a hustle.

One day my homegirl told me she had won an amateur night in Flint dancing at the strip club, $500! Now she was speaking my language .

I was extra confident that I would be able to go and win! And that's exactly what I did. I was amazed at how much money could be made in that industry and there I was, "Sunshine" was born! I had no idea the trouble I was setting myself up for. Integrity didn't matter because I didn't have any, Morals didn't matter because I didn't have any of those either. My mind was strictly on making money.

I became a regular " house girl" at the club. I didn't have much of anyone outside of my sister to keep my baby so I just started leaving him with just about anyone so I could go down there and make that money. Early mornings and late nights were my new norm, I was getting addicted to the lifestyle.

I was really confused as to which direction to turn. I was hopeless, daring and naive. Prime target for a slick talker.

And here comes… we'll just call him "Bobby Gray". I met him on a mild afternoon walking to my friend's house. He was charming and looked like he had money, not much else really mattered. I was out for myself, no time for the moral stuff. Our secret relationship progressed fast. I was his "cuddy buddy", "side piece" or whatever. He had a girl and I knew it; I had done much worse than be with someone who had a girlfriend.

He was always sweet to me and I was crazy about him. Everyone in the hood knew I was his girl except his girl. I went along with it because it felt like he was proud of me. That was a feeling I never had, not even from a parent and it felt so good! I let him parade around with me on his arm because I wanted to feel kept. I was low in spirit insecure and looking for love in all of the wrong places!

One day his girl found out and it caused a big scene in the hood, I'll never forget it. I stood there in a heated argument amongst the three of us. There were so many bystanders just trying to catch the drama. She and I argued back and forth about me and him. As expected he stood there and denied ever being with me! Although I knew we had an agreement to keep things on the low I got in my feelings! I still felt violated. My little heart was telling me that I loved him, why would he do this? I wanted him to pay for my feelings, even if it meant blowing his cover!

At that point I just wanted to be his Girl.

I didn't feel like I had anything to lose so why not act a little crazy?!

In the midst of everything I yelled out "You didn't say that last night!" that totally set him off! The next thing I know I took a heavy blow to my face in front of everybody! I was so embarrassed, and he was so UNBOTHERED by the fact he had just slapped fire out of my mouth!

He jumped in his black Cutlass Supreme and sped off!

I felt so ridiculed and embarrassed! I knew I did this to myself, why did I even have to say anything?

I swore to myself I wouldn't deal with him again. I couldn't believe how he had just played me and embarrassed me!

That attitude didn't last long, within hours he was calling with an apology begging me to take him back. He claimed he didn't know what else to do. I was naive, all I imagined was hearing him say he'd leave her and be with me. I was dumb enough to go along with it and of course you know what's next he was there that night! Typical abusive relationship.

Me and "Bobby Gray" were on again and off again for many more years. For some reason I couldn't shake him, and he couldn't shake me. I started new relationships, but He kept resurfacing in between each and every one of them.

In the midst of all of that I ended up going to jail. I really didn't have anyone to call on because everyone was pretty much tired of my mess.

I reached out to "Bobby Gray" he was already kissing up to me for the slap incident, so this was a great opportunity for him to get back in good graces. He was "Johnny on the spot!" He came to my rescue so fast! That was all I needed!

After all of my troubles no one ever ran to my rescue like that. I felt loved by him and there we were again in the mix of our Ghetto Love Triangle.

Somehow, I was still maintaining my apartment. After a while I got back in the swing of things and went back to the club.

It was a struggle trying to find someone to keep my baby on a nightly basis without leaving him with just "anyone". I took my baby to my uncle one night so I could party. That night turned into two nights. After he had him two days he called my mother to come get him. Two more days had passed and I still had not come back to get my baby. I still had not called to give anyone my whereabouts I had just pretty much took off to party and get high for four days. I loved my baby boy, but my party lifestyle had taken over and I was completely out of control!

My mom took care of my baby for two days, after those days went by she decided she could not care for him any longer. She had lifestyle issues herself and was also recovering from an accident. She felt like she couldn't care for my son considering both of their conditions. A call was made to Protective Services and they came and took custody of my precious 2year-old baby.

At that point I had finally came to my senses, it was time to check in and go get my baby, but that's when I learned it was too late.

My mind is gone! I couldn't believe what I had just heard. All I could do was ponder on it actually happening in my "mind's eye". I kept seeing them put him in a car seat. I kept hearing him crying for me.

After that all I could do was party and get high to get my mind off of things.

The incident with "Bobby Gray" and his girl in the hood had rumors chiming in the streets that his woman and her clique were going to jump me. I knew that was truth, I knew how they operated so every time I was in their neck of the woods I was prepared for what could have possibly went down.

One day my cousin invited me to an after-hours club, it was their spot. I knew chances of them being there would be very likely. I arrived at the party and there she is with five of her homegirls. It's just me and my cousin. I'm not exactly scared but I was definitely vigilant. I knew what time it was! They were going to fulfill their promise, their body language spoke loudly, I felt it my heart and I knew it was about to get ugly.

All of them looked as if they were waiting for the perfect opportunity. I didn't want to mess around, so I quickly decided it was time for me to get out of there! As soon as I approach the door I turn around and all five of them are following me.

My heart fell in My stomach! I saw one of my homeboys and I asked him for a ride but as soon as I opened the door and sat down all I could feel was someone pulling my arms and legs out of the car!

Just as I expected, they jumped me. Somehow I was able to pull my knife out. I had been prepared all night to do whatever I had to do if they executed the rumor I had heard on the street.

I was trying to get them all off of me, I was swinging my knife left and right not caring where or how anyone got cut. Blood everywhere and I'm in handcuffs, belligerent and causing a scene. I was so uncontrollable; I very distinctly remember the officer hitting me in the mouth with the flashlight and cracking my tooth. My lip was so swollen when I woke up that next morning... in the county jail.

Chapter 5

Hustle & Blow

Now I'm locked up, they had to sit me down. Honestly that's what I needed. My whole life was flashing before my eyes. How in the world could I have been so dumb?!

I was in love with the idea of being loved. I was hoping that perhaps one day I would wake up to him saying he wanted to be with me but that never happened and now I'm sitting in a cold jail cell waiting to see what is going to happen next in my life!
Things have got to get better from here!

I cut two of the girls several times and was convicted of felonious assault with intent to do great bodily harm counts A and B.

I was pretty much screwed! They had just taken my baby and I was supposed to be getting myself together to get him back, but matters were getting worse. I was going to take it to trial and claim selfdefense, but I kept having a sneaky suspicion my case wouldn't win and I'd go to prison so I might as well just plead guilty and do my time in jail.

My experience during incarceration was unreal, crooked deputies who were easily persuaded. I knew I was going to be there a minute and had to make the best of it. So, I took advantage of two of them that were a little "sweet on me". I knew I could get them to run me a few extras, nothing major but I definitely got special treatment. I had them bringing me everything from food to makeup to cigarettes and longer visits! They could've easily lost their jobs but clearly that wasn't a concern. I was angry at men, I always seemed to get the short end of the stick, so if this was my chance to have the upper hand and not be the one with something on the line, I'll take it.

I was obviously running from God but no matter where I went it was obvious he was there, even in jail!

Some of my "dorm mates" found out I could sing so there I was, the praise and worship leader at Ingham County Church of God! That responsibility made me go to chapel much more because I knew people wanted to hear me sing.

Court time comes and I plan to plead not guilty, running the risk of going to prison. Miraculously one of the girls dropped her charges! Yes God! I quickly plead guilty and was sentenced to one year in the county with good time I was out in 10 months.

Unfortunately, the state had only given me one year to get myself together and get my baby boy back it had already been several months before I had gotten locked up. That year ran out while I was serving my sentence.

I will never forget the gut-wrenching feeling I had when I walked out to the sally port to sign off my

A Wonderful Change

parental rights to my baby boy, who I affectionately called "Andy".

I was so sick to my stomach I laid in my cell all day crying and sobbing to the point that I could hardly breathe . Months later things were finalized with his foster parents to become his legal parents. I was no longer eligible to be my baby boy's parental guardian. There is no way to describe the feeling I had. I hated myself and the situation I was in! I had absolutely no hope and nothing to live for. My release day came but it wasn't a happy one.

You're talking about Clueless? I'm just going through life with no Direction! Scrambling to figure out which way to turn next, all while numbing the pain of my baby boy being taken away. The pain of not having him is literally taking all of my energy and drive. Some of my friends had done what I had done. If I left my baby with my family I thought for sure he would be right where I left him just how things operated in other families. How could I be so stupid? Just to party? This is the worst feeling ever.

Just upon my release from jail my father came back into my life. He had decided to move back to Lansing, and we began to develop more of a relationship. More than what we had spending time only at holidays. It looked like he was going to be around for a while. We didn't warm right up to each other immediately; it took time for us to act like father and daughter. I carried on just as I did before he came back.

I was trying to go about life as best as possible. I was numb to pretty much everything.

One day my friend introduced me to her uncle, he was relatively young maybe about 30 and I was 19 or 20. I thought he was fly he had a certain swag about himself.

We really hit it off in the beginning but as time moved on he became very controlling; I never really had a sense of direction, so I took it as he was showing me something in life. It felt like someone was "keeping" me. It didn't take me long before I moved in with him and his mother who was a local Evangelist in the area.

My new Man "Tee" knew I was dancing at the club, it was right up his alley, come to find out he was a straight-up pimp. His mother knew it and showed absolutely no expression of concern for what was going on in her house. I knew he had other girls, it should've bothered me, but I ignored it. It just felt good having somewhere to be and a little sense of family.

"Evangelist so-and-so" went along with it as long as we cleaned her nasty house. I'm pretty much acting out of ignorance and low self-esteem, clearly I had absolutely no value for myself at that point. I had no hope for change and couldn't fathom the idea of becoming the awesome woman of God which was ordained for my life! If someone had told me things were going to get better I wouldn't have believed them.

After learning he was a pimp I adamantly refused to "turn tricks" I just couldn't do it! Because of my stance, Tee became really violent! He would do things like lock me in the basement, push me down sets of stairs, kicking and punching me repeatedly at times.

Swinging around a pole was one thing but going far as being a street walker was beyond my thoughts.

He locked me in a room one day, his cousin stayed there for hours just to make sure I didn't come out of the basement if I did he threatened to beat me again.

I remember looking around the room in disbelief, my life was at an all-time low. How in the world was I going to get out of this mess?? This man always threatened to kill me if I left him, Lord please help your Girl, I need you now!

Depression was really starting to take hold of my life. I didn't want too much of anything, honestly I really just wanted to lay down and die. Eventually he came back to get me late the next day, I was hungry, weak and all cried out. He took me back to his Mother's house so I could get some rest, how sweet? NOT! I laid up for about two days I was completely drained, once I felt better I packed the small things I had and left one day while his Mother was taking a nap.

I felt better physically but mentally I couldn't compute why all of this bad stuff is happening to me. All I wanted to do was get really drunk and die. My friend came and picked me up one day, so we could go party. We were all getting drunk that night. I went in her friend's medicine cabinet and took every pill she had in there. Hours later my stomach was turning knots I was vomiting violently! I was afraid to go to the hospital because I had warrants! I called my best friend Janielle. It didn't take her long to come and get me, I was so high and out of my mind. I could hardly see straight. She took me straight to church for prayer! I fell out sobbing, my body was so weak, and the Pastor was praying continuously over me.

My friend invited me to her house that evening to rest and recover. I rested a while, but it wasn't long before I was back on the grind trying to survive.

I couldn't kick depression; I could not get over being without my baby. It was hard having no money and caring for him with his special needs, but I still wanted to be responsible for him, I knew I did wrong, I so badly wanted a second chance and die at the same time.

Every day I woke up I wanted to die. One day I went to my mother's house and figured I would try the pill trick again. I raided her medicine cabinet and took every pill I could get my hands on that evening. I was still resentful with her due to the situation with my son but honestly I created that storm.

I took the pills in a local Denny's bathroom; I was hoping to die in public so someone would find me quickly. According to first responders, I passed out unconscious with my face in my food. I woke up that next morning in a psychiatric hospital.

When I was finally able to open my eyes, I looked up and saw my aunt Roz. My stomach was so sore because they had to pump all of the medicine out. I was so embarrassed, depressed and in pain. As I laid in the hospital bed she just rubbed my head. She wasn't a woman of many words, but her presence meant everything! God rest her soul, she died a few years later.

Medication became my daily routine, I felt like they were trying to just give me a label. I was diagnosed with depression and bipolar disorder. They put me on just about every med you could think of. I began to feel unusual and very uncomfortable. I started seeing double and blurry visions. The atmosphere felt as if it was only a movie scene, people would run through the halls naked, sit all day rocking back and forth and of course just come up and cuss you out for no reason. I had to stay sane, I KNEW they were trying to justify the diagnosis. I had to make a conscious decision and avoid taking the meds if I didn't want to lose my mind. I started hiding them under my tongue. I think I stayed there for two months until I proved to them that I was no longer suicidal.

Back on the grind going back to the clubs. I knew it was an easy, quick hustle and everyone already knew me,

Waking up every day without my baby boy was completely agonizing. It heightened my psychotic thinking about suicide. That was the only time I felt crazy. I was completely fine until I started thinking of Andy.

I couldn't get my mind off of my baby boy!! I hated life and I just wanted to die!! I thought I would give suicide one last shot, I literally attempted it one more time!

I went to a hotel in the local Lansing area and decided this would be the night. I decided that I would get high, and drunk again, and try to blow my brains out. This time was more of a guarantee. I snorted a bunch of cocaine so I could be high out of my mind, enough to pull the trigger without thinking twice.

There I was on my knees in front of the mirror. I was resentful towards my mother and blamed her for my son being taken away, so I called her up so she could witness what was about to take place. I wanted her to feel the pain that I was feeling .

A Wonderful Change

There I was with a loaded Glock 9 to my head with the safety off I pulled trigger nothing happened, I continue to try to fire the gun and nothing would work I became so frustrated I started banging the gun on the sink counter with it facing me hoping that it would just fire by mistake! Nothing. The gun would not shoot for the life of me LITERALLY!

At that point I had a meltdown because I started to see that God would never let me end my life! The extreme times that I have attempted suicide never worked and this here was by far the most likely way of working and it still didn't work I knew right then, God was not going to allow me to die by Suicide, he was showing his mercy on my life.

My mother was freaking out on the other end of the phone. I could hear her talking to the police on her cell phone. At that point, every tear I could even produce came out of my eyes. I just laid on the floor crying, screaming, asking God why?! That was DEFINITELY my rock bottom! All I could do was cry and plead to God to save me from myself. I knew I really didn't want to die; I just didn't want to continue living how I was living.

The police came and evacuated the entire hotel. They kicked the door in and instructed me to put the gun away and walk out of the room backwards with my hands up!

There were police everywhere, more like SWAT team, men in black. All of them with shotguns drawn, masks and all kinds of stuff. I saw all of the police; I couldn't believe the situation I had caused and gotten myself into, so I just held my head down in shame.

I stood there as they handcuffed me; all I could do is cry. An officer paying close attention to my level of sorrow asked what was truly going on with me. I began explaining to him about my baby and how he had just gotten taken away and that he was my life. If I didn't have my son I just wanted to die.

The man said the sincerest thing to me, he looked me in my face and said, "Ma'am this isn't a crime, your hurting and you need help." They took me downtown for the investigation, confiscated the gun, did not charge me with any type of possession of the handgun and admitted me to another psychiatric hospital..

Here we go again, everyone was either hunched over or having frequent psychotic outbursts. I knew I was only depressed, and God would help me better than medicine. I felt like medicine would make me worse off, so again I hid the meds under my tongue.

I had to shake this generational cycle of depression and medicine wasn't the answer!

I stayed there another 2 months until I proved I was mentally stable enough to be back out in society and care for myself on my own. This time was different, with this being my second run in the mental health hospital my family was growing concerned. My cousin Tanya, and my friend Angela both came up to make sure I was alright while I was there. I remember them bringing me gifts, to take my mind off of things; that was good looking out. Although I was still depressed and suicidal I faked my wellness to the point that they finally discharged me.

Fresh out of the psych ward, homeless and no money. I needed a fresh start, so I went to Flint and worked at more little clubs.

I moved down there and stayed with a friend. A close family member dropped me off and I can still remember in my heart dreaming of them saying –"I won't leave you here, I will take you with me", but that didn't happen. It was hard to believe this person that I was born to and should've been protecting me just left me with a nasty old man to fend for myself. Great just great! But oh well let me get it how I live.

I had to maintain my hustle and working at the clubs was pretty much what I knew. The "old man" kept pressuring me for sex and I was NOT with it. I was grossed out every time he tried to pursue me, I knew I didn't want to share myself with this man and I also knew I would find myself homeless if I didn't. Chil' homelessness it was!

I got up out of there and started to couch-surf between a few people I had known from the clubs.

After a while the club DJ helped me get my own apartment. I had the best neighbors! They were all drug dealers , strippers & dope fiends. It was very convenient for the lifestyle I was embarking upon, by now powder cocaine had become my drug of choice.

There were two different sides when I was high. I either wanted to whip out the bible and talk about Jesus (God actually used me a few times when I was high) or I wanted to kill everyone in the house. There was no in between!

One night I was hanging out at the afterhours motorcycle club with one of the other dancers her name was Tiger. We let another girl roll with us, her name was Gina. She was alright, but loud and obnoxious. We only let he roll because she had dope for the night. We were at a ROUGH club, everyone had guns, dope and/or weed on the table, strippers were making money and chicken was being fried back in the kitchen! My girl Tiger was scared the whole time! She was a quiet girl from the Grand Blanc area which is a suburb on the outskirts of Flint.

Eventually we all left with Gina and dropped her off at home. All three of us had been getting high all night so anything was bound to happen!

Before dropping Gina off we started arguing amongst ourselves. We pulled up to her house and jumped out! She had probably six of her family members standing on the porch ready for something to pop off, meanwhile, it's me and Tiger and she was scared to death.

I'm "frozen", high as a kite, feeling on top of the world. It didn't bother me that I was outnumbered ..I was strapped with my little 22 and wasn't afraid to pop somebody.

Of course, we started fighting, thank God her family did not jump in! It was just me and her fighting in the middle of the street toe to toe! All of a sudden I felt the worst pain I had ever felt in my life! This chick had literally bit a chunk out of my face!

My homegirl was scared and stayed in the car the whole time! I saw all of that blood gushing out; it took everything out of me not to shoot her, but I was a hustler not a killer.

I ran to the car and we left! After sliding past prison for cutting those girls a few years back I knew I wasn't going to bust my gun so I knew I should just leave before things got worse!

My flesh was wide open bleeding profusely we didn't know what to do. Tiger thought of her friend who was an RN she rushed over that evening and put some kind of salve on my injury. It was too open and deep for stitches. I still have the scar to this day, it never healed properly, but it's all good because I'm alive to tell the story!

I couldn't work much or even at all at times because it took about two months for it to heal enough for it not to look nasty.

I had a special friend, I called him "Papa" who always looked out for me while I was down. He saved me from getting too far out with unpaid bills. When I was finally able to make it back to work I basically made money to "do me". I paid my bills here and there but for the most part I was "kept" by him. We had a lot of fun together, but he wasn't good for me at the time, he spoiled me in the worst way and my habit grew out of control. Suddenly we broke up, that was probably a good thing because he was "technically" "OFF LIMITS"!

I hated working at the club, eventually I stopped going, but that was my only hustle to keep things afloat, so my bills piled up really quickly. I sold everything I had for little of nothing at the last minute just to get back to Lansing and try to start over again.

Chapter 6

Sumthn' Like an Ike & Tina Remix

Of course, granny the one who I felt loved me most let me come back again! She knew I wasn't living right but she let me come back anyway.

It had been a few years since my Andy was taken away. At this point I'm just feeling unworthy, STILL didn't have my baby, I broke up with Papa, lost my apartment and everything I had only to come back to Lansing the place I hated most!

After a while I got back out in the streets, I started hanging with an old home girl, and we would party a lot.
One night we had a party and her boyfriend brought someone along with him to meet me.

I will never forget it; I was at her house sitting on the stairs when this big dude comes in behind her boyfriend… My heart fell to my stomach for some reason I felt the instant connection, they didn't even have to tell me he was the one coming for me!

He was fresh out of prison. Big muscles and a deep voice. I was in "love at first sight" ghetto edition.

He looked me in my face and said she's going to be my baby mama! Everyone started laughing but I'm sitting there looking like "This dude is crazy!" Make a long story short we quickly progressed into a relationship, months later I found out I was actually going to have his baby.

Things between us were never right. The first few months were ok but other than that things quickly started going downhill. He snorted cocaine too so that made two mentally unstable people trying to maintain a relationship.

I quickly learned he was abusive just like the other guys. He was more verbally abusive than anything. I was pregnant so he didn't put his hands on me, but he said things to me that hurt equally as bad as slapping me in the face!

I was called a whore and every expletive you could name every other day! He was driven by jealousy which started making him out of control!

The reality of being pregnant started to sink in I couldn't believe it; God was actually giving me another chance to be a mom! Andy, by now was four years old and it had been two years that we had been separated.

I was not sure what the state would say, and I was afraid for my new baby. I just knew they were coming to take my baby as soon as I had him.

I had to strategize and come up with something that would work, show them I had changed my ways and I was ready for Parenthood again.

I was determined not to let them come and take my baby! I had a lot of negativity in my ear, people around me who constantly reminded me to prepare to have my baby taken away, I was determined that was not going to happen.

Time to look for a job and work came easy because I had the gift of gab. I started looking for jobs I could do sitting down and found myself landing a telemarketing job. I was hired right on the spot. A legitimate job! I couldn't believe it; I was finally on my way up.

It was perfect, I was living with Granny, going to work every day and things were starting to come together for the good!

Meanwhile my relationship with "Baby Daddy" was getting worse, the further along I got in pregnancy the more controlling, jealous and now physically abusive he became. He started seeing other women right in front of me, it was no secret. I fell into depression again and the excitement of knowing I was going to have a baby with him had worn off.

He was known for his being the muscle of the crew and often called on to take care of the "dirty work". One day I was at a friend's house with him while they had a meeting. The agenda and the topics were way beyond my thoughts and abilities, I couldn't believe my ears! I was a thug but NOTHING on this level!

I was now back at the point of being torn between the "good girl" and bad girl" image. I knew I was about to have a baby and the thug lifestyle had to come to an end, and I hoped this also included an ending with my boyfriend. I loved the thug in him because I felt protected, but I also wanted to change and separate myself from anyone and anything that could make me lose my new child. At this point I just want to slow down and be a good mom.

Everywhere we went he had his gun; it was like he expected something to happen at any given moment. I vividly recall one time going to the store with his friend. I stayed in the car while they were running in for a second. Suddenly they both came out of the store and within a blink of an eye there was a shoot out! All I saw was gunfire being exchanged back and forth!! I was afraid for my life! I ducked down inside the car screaming, crying and praying! They jumped in the car and followed the car that shot at them first, they were STILL shooting! I was so shaken up, I begged them to drop me off. All I could think about was dying or getting shot in my stomach and losing my baby. I cried and pleaded for them to drop me off, when I got out of the car I looked back at the gun riddled car, my boyfriend and I separated with a kiss.

I was TERRIFIED! I couldn't believe what actually had taken place! I was paranoid on every level you could imagine. I thought the other shooters followed me to my drop off site. I thought the police were on our trail and looking for us. I thought I'd get arrested and have my baby taken. I was an emotional wreck. Later that night I watched the news and there was a segment about the shooting. The reporter stated that the mail carrier had been "grazed" in the leg by a bullet. I laid very low for several days until my paranoia subsided. Thank God, once again I felt covered by the blood of Jesus. Nothing ever came out of that situation. I should have left him right at that point, but of course not. We eventually moved on as if nothing had ever happened.

One day I snuck him in at Granny's house, he became upset with me because I had taken his cell phone. He was furious that I was looking through it and snatched it from me. When I got my hands back on the phone I threw it behind a big old-fashioned wooden chest of drawers which meant there was no way in the world anyone was going to be able to move it to get the phone! He became so frustrated he took out his gun and put it to my head and swore to shoot me if I did not get his phone from behind the chest of drawers! That was crazy!

My entire family was upstairs having breakfast. Somehow someway, I got that phone and got his behind right up out of there! He left in a rage...slamming the door so hard it seemed like the whole house shook. He shot his gun in the air and sped off with his friend who came to get him. That was so scary you would think at that point I would have left him alone but of course not.

I was fortunate enough to rent a small studio apartment it was pretty cute right in old town Lansing. I was still working and doing my very best. I had gotten my own apartment and invited him to come live with me. Now how dumb was that?

The time had come for me to give birth. There I was at the hospital. I had many family and friends there to support me. It felt good having so many loved ones

there. My labor time was quick, and I was ready to have my baby. My son's father was there high and smelling like weed in the delivery room. I wanted to fuss but I held my peace because Lord knows the first time I had a baby the daddy swore on his life that it wasn't even his kid, so I was just grateful to have this guy there and excited to see his first child born. A 7lb.
2oz healthy, bright eyed, baby boy.

Just as I anticipated Child Protective Services came up to the hospital to greet me. I was afraid but still had that mustard seed faith that told me to boldly stand up to them and fight for my son!

I told the CPS worker I was expecting her she couldn't believe it. I told them I knew they would come and investigate. I was well prepared for them to come and check me out, I had it all together! I looked forward to welcoming home my beautiful baby boy. They came and checked out my nice neat & clean apartment then petitioned the court to have my child come home with me.

I still praise God today and always will! They did not take my baby. However, they did enroll me in a program which was designed to have my parenting supervised for one year. I was also assigned a caseworker, we will just call him Mr. G.

By this time, me and my son's father had been in countless fights. Since I already had the baby I guess that gave him the okay to put his hands on me again.

I was so tired of the revolving door of abusive men I swore that the next one to hit me would get to see who I really was.

One day during a fight I got tired of him embarrassing me in front of everyone, tired of him putting his hands on me, tired of him disrespecting my family...I was just tired!! I picked up a kitchen knife and BLACKED out!! All I know is when I came back to my senses I had stabbed him 4 times! Blood was EVERYWHERE! My new baby was right in the next room. God knows I was playing with fire because CPS was already on my tail. I freaked out. I went and grabbed big towels to try and stop the bleeding. We sat in the floor both weeping and sobbing in disbelief at what had just happened. I was regretful and felt guilty. So guilty I felt like I deserved what was coming from him. He didn't lash back though, instead we went to the hospital and lied about the attack. He never accused me of anything, they patched him up and we went on with our crazy dangerous relationship.

Time went on, fight after fight. I had finally taken out a personal protective order on him and demanded that he stay away, we were equally abusive to each other. He should've had one on me as well!

One night I was sleeping in my living room with my baby boy cradled in my arms, all of a sudden a big brick came flying through my window, glass was everywhere! The brick fell just a foot away from the couch. He was paranoid, he swore on everything he saw a man come into the back of my apartment. He was insanely jealous, to the point I couldn't even maintain friendships with family members & friends. I was playing games with the personal protection order I would use it every time I wanted to break up with him. What a dangerous game to play. One day in a fit of jealous rage he choked me until my ears popped!! I experienced partial deafness for the entire day I WILL NEVER forget that! I should've walked away at that point, but of course not! Again, what a dangerous game to play.

My caseworker knew nothing of the relationship nor the abuse. If Protective Services had known I was seeing this guy and fighting like we were they would have definitely come in and taken my baby. To say we would only fight was an understatement. The abuses that we inflicted upon each other was like two gang members in the streets, everytime we fought there was blood shed! I can't claim to be the innocent one and I wasn't helpless either. We were mutually abusive. He would tear me up physically and verbally, I would tear him up with weapons.

I can't even count how many times I stabbed him throughout our relationship I will never forget the most memorable time. Something made me SNAP.....again! I remember picking up a ceramic object and breaking it on the table I gouged him on his shoulder with it! A chunk of his flesh came out and he started bleeding profusely. This time I was afraid for his life! Blood started trickling and squirting everywhere all over the wall. I had to run and get a big towel. It became extremely saturated with blood quickly and then he fainted. When he closed his eyes I just knew he was dead I started crying and screaming out to God that if he saved me from this situation I would not be with him again. This was a lie!

His stepdad came to get us that night to take us to the hospital. We were both afraid because there really was no way to explain how it happened. We could not lie our way out of this one. We were known by nearly every police officer in South Lansing for our domestic abuse. We knew if the police came I was going to jail. Looking back, we had the most volatile ghetto love/hate relationship!

He ended up coming home and I nursed his wounds to healing. It was such a bad injury there really was nothing to do about it, so they just had to let it heal which formed a serious keloid scar.

The fighting grew more and more intense! One day we were fighting, and he wouldn't get off of me! I didn't want to stab him after the fainting scare, I thought for sure the next time he wouldn't make it out alive. This time I bit him on his arm and with all of his strength he snatched away from me pulling my two bottom teeth out from the root! Blood just started gushing out of my mouth. At this point I am beyond rage it was almost as if I blacked out.

I used anything as a weapon I picked up a hot iron and burned him on the chest with it! I saw a boot with a heel I snapped and just beat him with all of my strength everywhere on his body even in his face I busted his head open and left him with a black eye. I had no control, I was furious! I was mad at the world, mad at men for how they had always treated me. It was his day to pay for it all, for every man who hurt me instead of protecting me.

The fight continued on. We were such a disturbance someone called the police and it went from there.

There was so much commotion! Thank God my baby was not there! surely Protective Services would have gotten involved.

I told the police he was the one who beat me even though the ambulance had already come and wrapped his head all around with white gauze, clearly he was bleeding in several areas of his face. I made the complaint and my teeth were missing so they immediately took him to jail, we both were guilty, but I was more of the aggressor in the situation. I will admit, I was wrong for a lot of the abuse that happened in that relationship I used his past as a way to justify what was going on(juvenile & prison record) but really I was just as crazy.

He never wanted to tell the police that I did anything to him even though it was obvious that I did. I guess it was some sort of "ghetto love" loyalty system we had going on, but he took one for the team and went to jail.

I let him sit there two days and conviction almost ate me alive. I finally had to call down to the police station and tell them exactly what had happened, I knew I was equally responsible.

Of course, they released him and charged me. I will never forget our reunion that night! You would have thought he was just returning from a tour in the military! We hugged and kissed, exchanged an "I love you" and went back home to our crazy, volatile and dangerous relationship.

Eventually I went to court. God's grace was still upon me considering everything I had done, I was only assigned probation and sent to anger management classes.

Somehow all of the domestic abuse and run-ins with the police slipped through the cracks. My case worker had no idea what was going on, in fact things were going so well with my job and my son he decided to petition the court and tell them there was no need for me to continue on with this program and I had progressed in such a way parenting supervision was no longer necessary. Shortly after that my case was closed, the surprise visits from Mr. G stopped and I never saw Child Protective Services again.

After every serious fight we would be good for maybe a month and then something would happen again. I was still working; we were still getting into fights. He was calling my job constantly harassing me. I broke up with him after he started acting crazy again.

Eviction followed and there I was, at the domestic abuse shelter...AGAIN. I was assigned an advocate; her name was Tracy. She was cool and always to my rescue in dangerous times, she always went above and beyond the description of her job duties.

Meanwhile my job is going good as ever and it wasn't long before I got a new apartment. I had just gotten a raise, and was using lots of resources through the state of Michigan. As a hustler while I wasn't going to do anything immoral or illegal, I did use what I knew to hustle the system! After being at the shelter for about two months I got a new apartment it was the best feeling ever. These bouts of homelessness were becoming too familiar, at this point it just felt good to be on the "up" again.

I moved in, everything is good and of course you know "Boyfriend" is sweet talking me! But the question was… "why am I STILL entertaining him"?

I would fall for it every time. It felt good knowing he was the father of my son; it was the only sense of acceptance I had sharing a child with someone. I had a low perception of myself and all I wanted was a sense of belonging. I overlooked everything negative about our relationship hoping things would change one day. I wanted my son to know what it was like to have both parents in his life.

I would invite him over from time to time but soon as he started acting crazy I'd run back to the personal protection order when I didn't want him around. We played so many games with that! He grew more into a stalker, calling my job more and more to the point where they were threatening to fire me, I was one of the lead marketers but that didn't matter. They were sick of the disturbance, honestly I didn't blame them. That was enough for me to analyze my situation. I had come so far, certainly I wasn't going to let this be the reason I lose it all, I was tired of losing.

I started staying away from him, but I had already let him know where I lived so he would show up at any given time I couldn't dare have company that was too risky! He was bound to show up, it never failed.

There were nights I'd be asleep, he would come in the middle of the night tapping on my window, calling and yelling my name. I was afraid and confused. I was afraid to continue on with him and confused about what my next move was, I had to lose this guy for good.

The last time he and I were together he stole my phone, so I didn't have a way to call the police if something happened. I planned with Tracy to get an emergency 911 phone from the domestic abuse shelter.

One day after work I was dropped off at home. I went in my room to get my son's stroller and there he was standing in my closet! Yes, he was hiding in my closet!
I took off running and yelling, he took off running behind me, it was the scariest feeling in my life! He jumped on top of me yelling for me to shut up! The neighbors came out, someone called the police but before they got there he left!

My neighbor took me over to the McDonald's where I met Tracy my advocate. She could not believe what had happened I was going to meet her to get a phone in the case of an emergency and the emergency had already happened right then!

That was the incident that took me out of the game. Of course, another eviction followed. I had to pack my bags and get up out of there.

In the midst of all of that drama I decided to have a girl's night out, I needed a break from everything that was going on.

I had just been evicted from my apartment, my son's father was constantly harassing me, and I just needed a break! I dropped my baby off and went to hang out with some of the homegirls. I still wanted to play around with cocaine, so I decided to get high for Old Time sake.

I really had no business doing powder again, it had been a very long time since I had gotten high, but I was stressed out and felt the need to get high. I will never forget the adrenaline rush I had that night, I felt on top of the world.

A girl rolling with us "cut into me" rather say confronted me about something simple. I really can't remember what the issue was, I didn't even know her before that night . She had met her match and I was ready to give her exactly what she was looking for.

The fight began inside of the house and ended outdoors. I was always stronger than the average woman my size so handling her was a piece of cake, even though she was a larger woman. We fought and fought, bystanders were everywhere. Someone broke the fight up and she left, so we thought she did.
She went to her van and came back to confront me; another fight broke out. We were all over the place! As a kid I loved wrestling and it was my time to play out some of those moves I learned!

I felt dripping on the side of my face, but I kept fighting, I felt something sharp, but I kept fighting. I was high and out of control, I just kept fighting. It all happened so quickly, and the house was dark. No one realized she had a box cutter in her hand, every time she contacted me she cut me! On the side of my face, my eyelid, on the side and back of my neck and on my foot(I was dragging her, and I was wearing sandals). This woman cut me 5 times! What I thought was sweat was actually blood. I ran into the bathroom and cut the light on. My eyelid was wide open, my whole face was bloody from the other places she had cut me, and my foot was hurting badly!

I had to go to the hospital and get stitched up. It had been a while since my "street" days, and I didn't have warrants, or any reason that I couldn't go to the hospital, it felt good knowing that I was about to go give them my real name and not worry about going to jail upon discharge. That might sound small, but I have learned to be grateful for the small things.

Here I am playing with fire again… fighting in the streets would be an easy way to be deemed "unfit". I had to make sure nothing like that happened again! It took quite a while to recover from that. I still have scars. But I am grateful for them. I'm grateful for the difference between a scar and a wound. A wound is still healing but a scar is already healed.

That situation taught me to "fall back" and focus on myself and my son. I had a second chance to prove myself and I knew I had it in me.

I didn't know why it was so easy for me to always get an apartment (nothing but God's favor) it wasn't long before I had another one . It was pretty nice too!

I went three months trying to stay away from my son's father, yet the first thing I did once I got set up was have him come over.

That night was like never before, it was like nothing bad had ever happened between us. He was trying his hardest to act like a new person and I was too but both of us knew we were not good for each other.

This time I let him move all the way in. This time he has a key! Of course, the abuse continues we were fighting left and right but the last time I stabbed him made me see how easy it could be to kill someone by accident, I refused to pick up a weapon! I had to get smart and use a weapon that would truly get me out of this situation.

I had always been taught to pray and develop my relationship with the Lord and that's exactly what I began to do. I knew I could not continue to live the way I had been living. It was time to make some changes. If I wanted to keep my son and live a peaceful life I had to create a new strategy.

I had a friend in Grand Rapids who always told me if I ever needed a place to get away from him that I can come and start over, staying with her and her family. She would tell me that all the time, but I never really considered it until the day came that I was truly exhausted.

Of course, I got the "baby please" speech on the days I threatened to leave. He actually picked up a construction job, making pretty decent money. He made promises to take care of our son and marry me, it all sounded good, but talk is cheap. I needed consistency but he had already blown the chance to show me. I wasn't going turn back again. I couldn't be more serious.

I'm leaving for good; I was still alive and so was he. I didn't want to chance it. I knew we would fight another time and that might have been the fight to take one of us out.

He left for work one morning and I moved out while he was gone.

I called my friend Candice and took her up on her offer. My son and I ran to start a new life in a new city. That was the end of a very long 3-year physically and emotionally abusive relationship. I never looked back to being with him from that day forward.

Chapter 7

Baby Steps.. I'm gettin' there

God is doing a new thing!(Isaiah 43:19)

Here I am in Grand Rapids Michigan a new city, new people, new opportunities! I wasn't in Lansing, but I wasn't too far, just right. This was exactly what I had been looking for. Candice lived in a beautiful community and I was able to transfer my job, there was an office in Grand Rapids. This was too good to be true!

I got settled in, I didn't have a car, but I learned to navigate the Kentwood and Grand Rapids area. My job was going great and I am making new friends. I was really enjoying my job, after a while I received a promotion and a raise. That was the best I had ever felt!

I was finally proving that I was able to be responsible for myself and my child. Look at me, growing into "my woman" I began to learn and love myself. I learned that I wasn't as angry as I let the world provoke me to be. I was soft, hard-working, energetic, fun-loving and domesticated. I started to view men differently. I saw them as worthy and full of value, but I also began to hold them accountable for how they treated me. I would no longer just deal with it or run. I chose to address my issue and give the other person a fair opportunity to respond favorably. If there was no remedy which made me feel like the Queen I had grown to know, I had to make a conscious decision to end the relationship. Those were my rules and I stuck to them.

Meanwhile I had gained the romantic interest of a guy whom I had met back in Lansing. I immediately grew a liking for him as we began to date regularly.

He was a nice guy with a nice car and job. This was a good start considering what I had just went through, everything else was negotiable.

I was getting anxious to move from my friend's house. She was a great help to me, but I was used to having my own. My son was getting to be a big boy, I was dating, and it was time to start looking for my own apartment.

A Wonderful Change

One of my friends at work helped me get a place down the street from where they lived, it was very nice and my son had his own room!

New city, new apartment, and a new man! I just knew for sure things were well on their way and I couldn't have been happier.

It had only been a couple of months; this new relationship had progressed fast…. (Story of my life). This was different..
he had asked me to marry him! I was flattered by the idea of stability and companionship. For so many years I felt like I wasn't good enough. I thought long and hard about it. I wanted to be married but I wasn't sure if it was him, so I deferred his offer until he was consistent.

His entire family loved me, some of them I had known from my childhood. But as time progressed his attitude started to change, and I was growing less and less physically attracted to him. "The honeymoon" stage was over. I was in love with his potential. The smallest thing would irritate me, he annoyed me greatly. Sometimes, just looking at him would turn me off. I was more in love with the idea of companionship and stability than I was with him. What a dangerous game to play, playing with someone's emotions!

One day my son came to me and told me that my boyfriend was being mean to him. He claimed that he pinched him and made him take a time out behind the couch. That was it! He was getting the boot! He wasn't on the lease anyway!! I told him to leave because I would not tolerate that behavior especially towards my son. That was definitely a deal breaker. I had been looking for a way out, and little did he know God had just provided it.

After everything I had already gone through, my baby was my second chance and I dare not let anyone or anything threaten him! My baby boy was a gift from God, I failed once but this was my opportunity to show that I would love and protect my child. He left and stayed in a motel. I had time to sort out my feelings. I didn't want some dude trying to be a daddy to my precious son. I was learning to be a good parent myself and didn't need that distraction especially if your struggling as a parent too. I just barely had it together, this "Good Woman" thing was new, and it was too risky bringing him in the picture with those red flags.

He was my only source of transportation, and that second income was gone, I had been through much worse than this. I continued my hardest, going to work every day whether I had to catch a bus or get a ride I was there and on time! My son was in preschool and wasn't missing a beat.

 One thing I was reminded of was what happened with my oldest son and I was determined not to let that happen again. I stayed on my grind and did my very best.

My momentum was still up and things were going excellent, better than before.

I took some time to readjust, focusing on me and my little one, finally enjoying life. I was still believing in love and I still aspired to have a healthy relationship.

I played around with the idea of getting back with Bobby Gray, but he was doing time in prison. I thought I loved him but really I was just in love with the idea of him loving me. He was bad news and I knew it. After a few letters I quickly got over him and his dreams he tried selling me. He never intended on being with me, there was no sense in believing his prison lies, it was time to finally close the book and stop entertaining his manipulation for good.

About six months into my new city, an old friend found me, it was "Papa". My old lover from my club days in Flint. I had a new mindset and didn't want to rekindle any old business, but he was getting my attention. I knew I was in a safe zone as far as abuse, but he was still off limits. We knew better, but busted that closed door wide open again.

He was so sweet to me, giving me everything I wanted. He was such a breath of fresh air!

This time around was different because I had a child. It took me a long while to allow him to meet my son. It was already a major change leaving his father who he knew. Then I started a new relationship with someone who was mean to him, so I was NOT about to have him meet someone else. All of our dating was done in secret.

He was a good provider, taking good care of us. There wasn't as much pressure on me and gave me a break not having to work as much, so I looked into going back to school.

Papa was articulate and professional; at times I was perplexed at the fact he even wanted to be with me. I didn't have much to bring to the table, other than my willingness to learn, loyalty and love. I also knew that giving that type of attention didn't make sense if he wasn't available, but he was special to me. I treated him well and that's all he wanted. I started falling in love with him. He wasn't just a guy I was having fun with. I truly loved him.
He began to encourage me to have more for myself.
He encouraged me to grow more independent yet still offering his support to lean on. Everything he encouraged me to do was to better myself and my son. He wasn't interested in buying my love, but he invested in my future, things no one could take away. No one had ever done that for me. We were both vulnerable and the attention we gave each other felt good, despite the mess we were creating.

I really started to pay attention to how he was encouraging me, and then the light bulb went off! He was right about all of the positive things he said about me. I knew it was time to align with all of the compliments he gave me because I believed it!

He often said things like... "You're a Queen" " You're someone's wife" "You're so intelligent!".

I'm beginning to see my own worth and it was just fuel to the fire burning inside of me! At this time, I'm somewhere around 26 or 27 years old, and believe it or not I hadn't even learned how to drive so that was the first thing I did.

Just as soon as I learned how to drive he bought me a car as congratulations with MY name on the title! I was too excited and definitely could not stop there I knew I had to finish my education, quietly as it was kept I had to reveal to him I had not graduated high school. I was so embarrassed, but he didn't flinch! He said…"What are we waiting for?!"

So, I quickly enrolled to obtain my G.E.D.! I knocked those tests out without the classes. I couldn't believe it! I impressed my own self! At this point I'm high on life, I'm starting to see the light at the end of the tunnel.

I still couldn't stop there, so I pondered on what industry I really believed I could thrive in. I knew I was good at sales but that really wasn't my passion I wanted to be some sort of businesswoman and run an office. I had never done that before, but it was burning inside of me. I wanted to wake up, get dressed in business attire and head to my office!

I decided to enroll in a local Institute where I acquired my medical administrative certificate and later the National Career Readiness Certificate. It is the equivalent to an associate degree.

There were thousands and thousands of employers looking for people who had that certificate and now I was one of them. How exciting!

I had never made this type of progress in my entire life. I started attending a small church at the end of my road and other churches around the city. It was time to get my faith back in line. I was seeing prayers answered and my dreams were coming true.

As things are at an all-time high they quickly plummeted to an all-time low. My granny had fallen deathly ill. It broke my heart to pieces!! All I ever wanted was for her to see me come out of all of the hardships she had experienced with me.

The last time I saw her we had a very good talk. She told me I was shooting straight to the top! Those words are still buried in the deepest part of my heart, shortly later she passed. That year was 2007. Although my heart was broken by her death, I was glad she saw me make progress, she was always confident I would do well. Granny was my loudest cheer leader.

I'm slowly understanding my worth, I knew if I continued this relationship I would not experience the fullness of what God truly had for me. I had to be real with myself, Papa wasn't available for me exclusively and I knew it When it came to love and family I was willing to risk letting him go. I didn't want to be "tied up" when true love actually presented itself. I wanted to be ready and free whenever true love found me. It was time to end this love affair. He needed to face his issues. Things were looking up for me and I didn't want to complicate it.

I went to him and cut everything off, I couldn't do it anymore. I started to realize I WAS someone's wife, that I AM intelligent and all of the things he had told me before! I never meant to use his encouragement against him, but I knew my worth. We were playing with fire, and I wasn't getting burned.

I knew it was going to be a struggle, but I was willing to take that risk if it meant I would have peace in my heart.

Chapter 8

A Wonderful Change

New Beginnings! For the first time in my life I am completely self-reliant. Financially things were pretty tight, but it felt good to know I didn't have to cut moral corners to make ends meet. No one wants to be the "side piece" when you can be the "main course"!

Just me and my baby boy trying to make it in Grand Rapids Michigan, still holding down my job, barely paying my rent but I knew things would begin to look up as long as I stayed focused and trusted the Lord to be my portion. Although I was loving my new life I started traveling back and forth to Lansing again. I wasn't in a relationship and wanted to rekindle things with both of my parents. By that time my relationship with my father had blossomed, it was as if we always had a great relationship. He was dedicated and really put in work to show interest in me and his grandson.

It wasn't before long I moved back to Lansing; a place I swore I would never return. This time it was different. I had a new mindset, and was determined not to let the things which had happened in that town take a toll on my success. Places I went triggered bad memories; faces I saw gave me anxiety BUT I refused to be paralyzed by fear! I kept running my race with full speed towards victory. I wasn't looking for love, I was only preparing to be found.

It seemed like everywhere I went someone was asking me out and for the first time I really didn't want to be bothered. I needed time to heal from everything I had gone through. Men were the cause of my pain...not the cure. I guess that was some pep talk I gave myself to make me feel strong. Because

A Wonderful Change

before I could blink an eye; I'm back in a relationship. He was incredibly sweet to me just as the last man I had dated because he WAS the last man I dated.. wait a minute?? WHAT?? Yes, it was Papa, and his name is Mark. He was still professional and charming, just like back in the day. However, now he was in transition, and available. He really didn't have much other than his business and his main job. I didn't have anything, not even a job. I was staying with various family members trying to figure out my next move. I knew Mark was worth it, I wanted him to see my potential. He had a few issues and a lot of baggage but compared to my mess it wasn't intimidating.

He and I chose to pursue a life together. He proposed marriage and I accepted! That's right! I'm engaged to be married! Not just engaged but being asked by a good man! Of course, the news got out fast. We had some haters, but we also had congratulators...either way we were getting married! I couldn't believe it; it was almost too good to be true. I was so glad I denied both previous proposals from my past.

For years the enemy would whisper lies in my ear. Telling me I would never be good enough for marriage and I'd always be a "side piece" I wasn't even good enough to be a mother so surely no one would purposely choose to spend the rest of their life with me. The devil was trying to steal my joy and kill my self-esteem. All of my life he tried to take away the little bit of confidence I had. As it turned out the devil is a liar! There were many challenges to face. My fears and guilt from the past. There was much to be ironed out with both us, we both had baggage, but we also helped each other unpack.

The first challenge I wanted to conquer was to ask God to forgive me for hurting others on my journey. Of course, it wasn't going to come easy for me, there were so many obstacles and hurdles.

Before long my past began to haunt me!

Family members began to whisper in Mark's ear about my past, things which they thought would turn him completely away from me! His situation was complicated as well, but what no one knew was that we had an open and honest relationship. We knew everything about each other ,the worst of the worst. I knew I was in a judgement-free relationship; I was with someone who truly loved me and wanted to see me blossom into the woman God promised I would be.

This new relationship felt so good. I now had the ability to sharpen my homemaking skills. He afforded me the opportunity to abort employment and make a home. Almost overnight I turned into this classroom mom, field trip chaperone, recipe experimenting, homemaking woman!

Although life was at an all-time high, I was still riddled with guilt knowing I was responsible for some of the dysfunction in his life. I deepened my prayer life and my relationship with God. I repented and asked God to put mercy in my heart so that I could forgive those who wronged me, and allow others to have mercy on me.

I just had to praise and honor God for what he had done in my life. I would often look back, walk down memory lane and fall down in Praise thinking of his goodness and how much he had saved me from!

I knew I had to return to God, but the difference was having a relationship with someone who wanted to seek God with me. It was beautiful, the feeling of praying with someone, worshipping with someone and serving God as a team! The feeling of setting aside every weight was so liberating, every burden was on the altar. No matter the judgment we faced from our past, we knew we were serving an all merciful God.

I knew if things were this good trouble might be around the corner! Especially if I had chosen to give my life back to the Lord!

I was right!

It was a Hot August day; Mark had left with his son to go look at tree care work. He was casually dressed in very comfortable clothing with the expectation of returning very shortly.

An hour later I get a call letting me know they had just been in a horrible accident! My whole life flashed before my eyes. Immediately, I thought the worst and I began pleading to God not to take my soon-to-be husband and his son! Praying and pleading that he would spare their lives. I wanted him to see how I was going to impact his life; He could not die!

I was finally on my way to love, peace and stability, it would be a terrible blow for God to snatch all of that away from me before I could even get a taste!

I rushed to the scene of the accident sure enough it was absolutely horrible! I recall seeing his truck flipped upside down crushed to the ground. There he was in an ambulance across the street head swollen two times its size, he was bleeding profusely I tried my best not to be too excited because I knew in a traumatic situation he did not need drama. I rode in the ambulance all the way to the hospital just praying and pleading to God to heal him and to block whatever the enemy had planned on his life! I was so afraid, but I just kept praying.

We are blessed to say he was victorious in God! He came out with injuries, but he is living strong & healthy today!

Mark had some limitations due to the injuries he sustained in the accident, he needed help and I wanted to be the one, so I became his assistant in his business.

I didn't know what in the world I was doing! All I knew was I wanted to prove to him that I would be the exact help he needed to keep business moving forward in a positive direction!

Overnight I instantly became his Administrative Assistant. I was taking calls, setting appointments, and driving him to look at work and all! I even developed a website! Looking back, it was horrible and looked like a first grader created it, nonetheless I just wanted to prove to him that we were indeed a team!

Chapter 9

Make It Last Forever

Wedding bells are ringing! Yes, you heard it right, Wedding Bells Are Ringing! I could not believe it, the time had finally come September 26th, 2010 the day we were to become husband and wife! Even though my past was on the forefront of my mind, I constantly prayed in my heart for forgiveness. The last thing I wanted to do was pay for it in my marriage.

That was truly the best day of my life I was finally breaking into my most sought after promises from God! Despite the lies the devil told me before, I'm getting married!

My father walked me down the aisle, he was prepared to hand me over to the man of my dreams! A man who had promised to protect me and never hurt me, a man who had promised to keep me and never leave me! A man who promised to provide for me and never leave me needy! I felt like the most blessed woman alive! That day was absolutely beautiful, a small very private, wedding...just as I had imagined!

We quickly progressed into our marriage; business is booming and my young son is getting to be a big boy!

A Wonderful Change

He embraced my boy just as if he were his own. At times it was hard to tell that he was not his natural son just by the way they connected and respected each other. I was blessed to have a man love and bond with my son, he needed a Father.

There was still a sharp pain in the deepest part of my heart, I had a 15-year-old son out there who didn't even know me! How could I be this happy about success in life when the greatest opportunity I had I seen as a failure? I often thought of him. Wondering if he was alive? If he was alive did he live in Lansing? What did he look like? Wondering if his family truly loved him and treated him right? Wondering if God would ever reconnect me with my baby boy, so he too could enjoy this wonderful life God has blessed me with? I almost drove myself crazy pondering on these things. I clearly recall Mark encouraging me not to use the word "if" but replace it with "when". You see "If" was a word to use when you are unsure, and "when" is a word to use when you are expecting something. I quickly changed the phrase "If Andy comes back" to "When Andy comes back!".

I stayed hopeful and faithful in prayer. I was expecting my son to return but God had a BIG surprise in store first. It was time for us to expand our family in a different way. Just three months into our marriage we found out that we were pregnant!

You talkin' about Joy??? I remember running all through my house praising God and shouting, I could not believe the news! Not only did God give me this wonderful man to share my life with, who accepted my son as his own, encouraged me to look forward to the day where my oldest son would return but now we will be welcoming a new baby into our marriage!

Come on Jesus! Won't he do it! I was on cloud nine you couldn't tell me anything!

September 19th, 2011 just one week shy of our firstyear anniversary we welcomed a bouncing 7 lb. 10 oz baby girl! She was so beautiful actually nothing that we imagined. She exceeded our expectation she was healthy, beautiful, strong and resembled both of our mothers very much.

Even with having a new baby I knew I had to continue on the path to my career and success with his business. I wanted to continue proving myself to him, letting him know he had made the right choice for a life partner to help him fulfill his dreams. I also wanted him to know I TRUSTED his leadership even though he had made mistakes in relationships and marriage prior to me. We were a team helping each other rebuild our lives. I am embracing my new position as his assistant. I'm constantly throwing out ideas and he is actually considering some of the strategies and ideas. Anyone who knows me can attest that I am idea-driven, they may not all be great, but I keep them flowing.

Before I knew it he began adopting my ideas and the business began to grow. We were also growing spiritually. It was time to rededicate our lives to the Lord! Yes God! No judgment from man mattered, what had been done in our past was in our past. We were walking in freedom and forgiveness.

Our expansion included a bigger house and even our own business space. We were blessed with a home twice the size of the one we had and business space less than 5 miles away. It was so hard to believe but I knew the promise God had on my life, I was even blessed with my first employee. The progress I had made was mind blowing, I'm finally living out my prayers and dreams.

Things are taking off! I began to put my brain power to optimal use. We began to acquire more equipment and tools. Eventually there was a complete restructure to the business and guess who became a legal partner? Me! I felt like my time and commitment was really starting to pay off.

Not only did he trust me to work for and with him but now he is sharing the actual business with me. That was enough fuel to give it my best... 100%. I felt that was only in my wildest dreams I would, or could become a business owner, this venture is going to be exciting!

The purpose of this business was to teach a trade to young people and others who wanted to acquire the skill of tree care. It was always important to him to encourage people to work with their hands. For years WiseMan Tree Experts has employed numerous people in the community helping to teach them a new trade they could carry with them for the rest of their life.

I needed to get to a certain understanding to do better business, especially now that I was a partner.

I knew my mentality, so a 2-4-year program wasn't going to cut it, that was more than I wanted to juggle while running a business and having young children, but I still needed those skills and tools right then.

I became a member of Fred Pryor Seminars. They offered Human Resource tools at their seminars which helped me be more effective and efficient in my position.

It was unreal, most times I would walk into the seminars with so much knowledge from studying on my own. Most other attendees thought I had my business degree just like them. There I was, with no degree raising my hand every time they had a question to be answered I would answer it knowledgeably.

They thought I was showing off, that I was some smarty pants. I was just glad to be amongst them. Glad to be making a positive contribution to society and glad to be in an environment much different from the hardships I had experienced before. I left every seminar with continued education credits to apply to a business degree just like everyone else.

Chapter 10

A Family Reunion

Singing ♪" A family reunion... it's a family reunion♪!" My God the promise had been fulfilled!

I will never forget, it was a hot sunny summer day July of 2014... I was sitting at my desk and I got a call from a lady I had not seen in over 15 years. Immediately I knew there would be lots of substance from this call, it's always something when people have to look you up.

She began to tell me that she was sure she had located my Andy, immediately I did not get excited because someone had shared that information with me before and the door was slammed in my face. I was totally denied a chance to pursue him. In an effort to protect my heart I tried my best not to get overwhelmed or too excited. She began to share details about this young man she saw at a military camp for youth, the details were so spot-on.

She even said he looked just like me!

I began to believe every word she said. Before I knew it she had provided me information to reach out to the young man who was indeed my long-lost son. We had been separated….. but now? I had finally found my beloved first born son.

All I could think of was him day after day. I took the information and reached out to the camp. They told me right away that because he was under the age of 18 he would have to get consent from his adoptive parents. I can't lie at that point my faith started to dwindle all I flooded my brain with was the "what ifs".
What if they never told him he was adopted? What if they don't want him to reunite with me? What if he has no interest in me. All of these things began to flood my mind and heart, but I stood strong and rebuked all of that nonsense in the name of Jesus! After all,.. "if God be for me, who could be against me" (Romans 8:31b NASB) right?

I pursued the situation with confidence and before long his adoptive parents had given consent that we could write each other.

My first letter from my son was so intriguing. He told me he always knew he was adopted, that his parents shared that with him when he was younger, and they promised to help him find me as soon as he turned

18. He told me he often dreamed of me and tried to imagine what I looked like.

My heart was so full! I don't think my heart had ever been that satisfied. From that point on I could not wait any longer to wrap my arms around my baby boy!

For a span of one month we faithfully wrote each other letters. I sent so many pictures of the entire family. He would write me and tell me things like I was so beautiful, that his sister was a cutie pie and he could not wait to meet her and his younger brother. He also promised to respect my husband and refer to him as his Dad. This was too good to be true!

Before long he had graduated his program and came to live with us. Once again a promise fulfilled from on high.

God sent me my son! He embraced me and the family with so much love!

Our bond was so natural it was hard to believe that we had once been separated for 15 years! This was a young man who had no recollection of me as his mother yet loved and respected me with high regards!

This was definitely a prayer answered and a dream come true!

It wasn't long that he adapted right into the family. He quickly acclimated to how our household functioned and started working with us at WiseMan. He also began taking classes at a local community college. He was on the Dean's list his very first semester!

This was definitely a miracle; I had only seen this type of stuff on Lifetime movies.

The man and woman who had raised my son from the age of three had even embraced me! Often referring to me as family. I began to develop a wonderful relationship with his mom a bright and loving spirit who told me she promised to help him find me when he became of age.

She and I became very close having frequent conversations on the phone. After a while I found out she was quite ill and bedridden, that explained why she was always hesitant about meeting me. That didn't bother me. I knew she was very sick and dealing with things her own way. I did what I could do to help her. I'd take her meals as often as I could to give her faithful husband some relief who cared for her hand and foot, day and night!

Very sadly she became deathly ill with just days expected to live.

Andy and I were on our way to lunch when her husband called us to rush up to the hospital! We busted a U-turn and rushed to her side. Just six months after my beloved son had reunited with me, the mother he never had, he was preparing to lose the mother he always had. What a sad time…

I was there for my son every step of the way, sitting in the hospital with my arms wrapped around him, his heart was broken and so was mine. God promised us that the tears we cried would be replaced with joy. I held on to that promise.

Alice (His Mom) passed away March 24th, 2015. That was so hard for my son Andy, his behaviors began to change, and it seemed as if he was backing away from me. I knew I ran a tight ship; my rules were strict, and my kitchen got pretty hot but certainly I did not want to push him away.

I wasn't sure if he just wanted to be close with that side of the family during this sad time or if it was me. The situation resulted in him moving out and going to stay with his grandmother.

As it turned out living with his grandmother seemed to be a better choice for him. Things happened so quickly, we jumped right into our family relationship which was a drastic change which called for a lot of adjusting.

It was sad for me that he moved out but truly it was a blessing for his grandmother who is getting up in age and needed someone to be there with her, so she didn't have to live alone.

She had always been a complete blessing to my son, you could see it in their relationship.

On the onset it looked like I had lost my son all over again, but God knew what he was doing, perhaps that was a mechanism used to keep us in good fellowship. Perhaps my parenting ways would have become overwhelming which could have pushed him away. He was still working with us, so I saw him every day at the office. He would come over as much as possible throughout the week and on the weekends. It was still a winning situation.

DeAndre (Andy) is so loving, gentle and kind. He even has a jovial spirit which reminds me of myself so much. He loves me unconditionally and I am truly blessed to have him back in my life. Words cannot explain the joy I feel; I have reaped the promises of God! My prayers ANSWERED; a promise fulfilled!

We are continuing to grow; our baby girl is getting bigger and our middle son is getting older. At this point we're outgrowing our home; it was time to step out on faith and receive our increase.

We went every direction to find a bigger home it seemed like denial sat on the footsteps of everywhere we went. We put off our search and made the best with the home we had. The house was too small for our family size but in obedience we began to wait on God to bless us with what he wanted us to have!

A Wonderful Change

One day I was at the office and I overheard my husband up front giving someone all of our personal info from income to social security numbers, it made me inquire as to whom he was providing all of this information to. He assured me that this conversation was private, and he wanted to see if he was eligible for a veteran's loan for a home. After the long periods of homelessness I experienced, I didn't care if he gave out my blood type and fingerprints!...I could just smell a home of our own.

I sat there with my ear glued to hear how this was all going to turn out.

I sat there for probably an hour imagining us in our very own home. A home that would provide room for us to continue hosting family gatherings. A home that I could practice "do it yourself" projects. A home in which I would provide the best nurturing I possibly could to my family, they deserved it.

It didn't take long before we heard the words "you're approved!" It was the week of my 36th Birthday and I was so excited!

I thought about all of the beautiful homes I used to admire as a young adult. I always imagined owning my own home. I would pay attention to the types of people who would enter and exit the beautiful subdivisions. Some driving beautiful, high end cars. I wanted my share of the "American pie" too!

We searched high and low for a great home, finally after looking at 5 or 6 homes, I walked into this particular one and on the onset I KNEW it was the home God promised me, I could just feel it. I felt right at home!

The price of the home I chose exceeded our budget by several thousand dollars, but my little heart was still convinced it was mine.

I encouraged the agent to talk the sellers into lowering the price, but my agent wasn't confident enough to do that at first. His exact sentiments were… "I've been doing this 20yrs and I've never seen anyone come down that much".

Immediately I had to testify about a God I knew who could do ANYTHING! He didn't know the God I was expecting to work this out had already delivered me from a lot of stuff, this was not too big to ask. Nothing is too big for God and this little situation was a piece of cake, if it be in his will.

It was a Wednesday night; we were leaving bible class when I received the call. The sellers decided to lower the price of the home and even pay our closing costs! You can't tell me God isn't good! What a miracle! His favor has always been on my life!

On May 9th, 2016 we were blessed with keys and a deed to our very own home! It was one of the happiest days of my life! There I was pacing back and forth in front of this beautiful home I used to only daydream about.

After being homeless most of my life and bouncing to and from substandard housing, this was surreal, so hard to believe. God was with us all of the way through.

It seems like with every blessing there is hardship around the corner because the enemy does not like to see God's people blessed!

Aside from the home being what we desired, another reason we chose the home and area was to be close and help my mother in-law who was a full-time caregiver to my father in-law, a 20-year stroke survivor with major limitations. Sadly, he passed away shortly after we were fully moved in and settled. On top of that my brother fell severely ill. Shortly after laying my father in-law to rest I received a frantic call from a nurse at Rutgers University Hospital in Newark, New Jersey. My brother was being rushed to emergency surgery after his aorta had completely separated from his heart!

What a bittersweet point in my life!

As I am basking in joy of our new home, my heart is broken by my father in law's death and the news of my brother being in a life-threatening medical situation had me torn!

This was my only brother. I knew I had to come to the rescue, he had been there for me in trying times and this was a great opportunity to show him his little sister had his back. My family and I packed up our vehicle and got on the road and drove 12 hours to Newark, New Jersey. When I got to the hospital I could not believe my eyes there was my brother laying there unconscious with tubes connected everywhere to his body. His body was swollen twice it's normal size and he was on life support.

I just knew for a fact he was on his way out. Sadly, my faith began to dwindle but I had to hang in there. I kept reciting promises of the Lord, I touched my brother from his head to his feet and proclaimed healing and victory in Jesus' name! I did not want to leave his side, but I knew at some point we had to return to Michigan, continue with business and kids' school. I could not let the support stop there! Two weeks later my husband and I jumped on a plane and went back down to check on my brother, at that point he had been HEALED! He had regained consciousness and was in recovery doing very well. I was shocked to see how much he had progressed! He had a tracheostomy and was moving very slow, he appeared to have lost a lot of weight nonetheless he was alive and well on his way towards healing! The difference in his condition from when I saw him last was NOTHING short of a miracle! God is so faithful, to this date two years later he is alive and well back to work and functioning in good health!.

EPILOGUE

Victory is mine! We are within the first year of serving at a new church! God had truly taken us through a growing process! We had grown to a point of taking on leadership roles in different Ministries.

One of which being the church Marriage and Family ministry. Who would ever think that we would be leading this type of ministry? It surely isn't that we have all of the answers, but we have been willing to do the Lord's work and share with others as we acquire wisdom from Heaven. Anything is possible when you believe in God. He is a God full of grace, mercy, redeeming & all transforming power.

Ephesians 1:7-8 says "In Him we have redemption through His blood, the forgiveness of sins, according to the riches of His grace which He made to abound toward us in all wisdom and prudence."

I am forever grateful that I have been saved by God's grace and transformed by the renewing of my mind.

Mark and I continue to serve each other, our family, our church and community in love, Faithfully!

We've had some rocky roads and hills to climb but God had been with us all of the way through.

My Husband Mark, to this day is one of the very best things that has ever happened in my life! He has stood by my side 100%! My lover, protector and very best friend. Our business is continuing to grow in a positive direction but none of that compares to who we have grown to be in Christ!

I've learned that my struggle was not for myself but to magnify the power of God! He had to use me to show others exactly what HE can do, so they also may grow in hope, faith, seek transformation and salvation. My greatest ambition is to encourage others to never give up, dream big, and put God first. You can do ANYTHING with his help! I will continue to live a life to inspire others.

I don't claim to have "made it". No one on earth has actually "made it", we go from grace to grace. There will always be a need for improvement and deliverance.
We should all keep striving towards our TRUE identity in Christ, no matter what lies in our past! "Nay, in all these things we are more than conquerors through him that loved us" Roman's 8:37 (King
James Version)

About the Author

Dara Mayhoe (Larkins) is a former street hustler and convicted felon who turned her life around to become a family woman, ministry leader, business owner, philanthropist and now Author. Her ambitious drive has allowed her to use her testimony as a way to help others build hope in God, and inspire those who seek positive change. She is a native of Lansing Michigan.

For Speaking engagements contact Dara at

larkwatts@live.com

Made in the USA
Monee, IL
24 September 2021